Introducing Dickens

Alex Madina and Valerie Lynn

CAMBRIDGE
UNIVERSITY PRESS

PUBLISHED BY THE PRESS SYNDICATE OF THE UNIVERSITY OF CAMBRIDGE
The Pitt Building, Trumpington Street, Cambridge CB2 1RP, United Kingdom

CAMBRIDGE UNIVERSITY PRESS
The Edinburgh Building, Cambridge CB2 2RU, United Kingdom
40 West 20th Street, New York, NY 10011–4211, USA
10 Stamford Road, Oakleigh, Melbourne 3166, Australia

First published 1999

Printed in the United Kingdom at the University Press, Cambridge

Typeset in FF Scala 10 ½/14 pt

A catalogue record for this book is available from the British Library

ISBN 0 521 599563 paperback

Illustrations by Chris Molan (pages 7, 8, 20, 28, 36, 40, 48, 59, 74, 79, 82, 84, 90, 95, 100, 108, 112,
116, 120, 122); Adam Stower (pages 34, 51, 68, 86, 88); and Sarah Young (pages 12, 14, 56, 104, 105,
106).
Cover illustration by Adam Stower

Acknowledgements
The publishers would like to thank Catherine Madina for her additional material and help in the
preparation of this edition.

p.13 'Money' by A. S. J. Tessimond from *The Collected Poems of A. S. J. Tessimond* with translations
from Jacques Prévert edited by Hubert Nicholson (White Knights Press, 1985) reprinted by
permission of the University of Reading.
p.105 'The Highwayman' from *Collected Poems* by Alfred Noyes, reprinted by permission of John
Murray (Publishers) Ltd.

CONTENTS

CONTENTS

Great Expectations: A Tale with a Twist

A Tale of Two Cities: A Swashbuckling Yarn

INTRODUCTION

This selection from Dickens' work is one of the Cambridge School Anthologies series and has been written for students and teachers who want to engage with literature in an active and varied way.

The selection is intended to show you his characteristic techniques and styles, as well as to introduce you to as wide a variety of his themes, characters and places as possible. The five novels we have chosen will, we hope, appeal to you on different levels.

First, *A Christmas Carol* is a text which you will almost certainly have heard of, read or acted. We have tried to introduce you to the themes of greed, miserliness and improvement as well as to give you an idea of the story. *Oliver Twist* is also well known, and we have tried with our activities to deepen your understanding of this tragic, dark novel. We have looked on *David Copperfield* as an engaging story of childhood, and *Great Expectations* takes the hero up to young manhood. Finally, *A Tale of Two Cities* is Dickens writing at his most masterly – a vivid adventure story set during the French Revolution.

You'll find that some of the episodes are quite short; others are several pages long. The text is printed on the right-hand pages, interspersed with activities on the left. You can work on the activities individually or in pairs or groups. Our directions are simply suggestions which should be altered to suit your needs. You do not have to do all the activities; they are simply our ideas for ways of becoming actively involved in the text.

We hope that you will enjoy this selection of key passages from some of Dickens' better-known novels. We have tried to include enough of each of the stories for you to follow the main sweep of events, but of course the best way for you to engage with Dickens is to read the novels themselves. Enjoy them!

Alex Madina and Mary Berry

A CHRISTMAS CAROL

An Eerie Ghost Story

1 A leaving present (groups of four)

Imagine someone is leaving your school or office and it is your turn to organize a collection for their present. They are not popular and everyone you ask has a different excuse for not contributing. Improvise the scene.

2 Portrait of a miser (pairs)

Dickens gives a very clear description of Scrooge to open the novel. Read pages 7 and 9 and discuss how he builds up a picture of Scrooge. Create a spider diagram similar to the one below to structure your thoughts.

What his voice and appearance suggest
*Scrooge has a 'pointed nose' which is pinched.
This suggests ...*

How he responds to others
He watches his clerk as if he is afraid he will be cheated ...

SCROOGE

How others react to him
Even guide dogs pull their owners away as if ...

What Dickens suggests about Scrooge's personality
The list at the opening describes him as 'a squeezing ...' This suggests ...

Portrait of a Miser

Oh! but he was a tight-fisted hand at the grindstone. Scrooge! a squeezing, wrenching, grasping, scraping, clutching, covetous, old sinner! Hard and sharp as flint, from which no steel had ever struck out generous fire; secret, and self-contained, and solitary as an oyster. The cold within him froze his old features, nipped his pointed nose, shrivelled his cheek, stiffened his gait; made his eyes red, his thin lips blue; and spoke out shrewdly in his grating voice. A frosty rime was on his head, and on his eyebrows, and his wiry chin. He carried his own low temperature always about with him; he iced his office in the dog-days, and didn't thaw it one degree at Christmas.

External heat and cold had little influence on Scrooge. No warmth could warm, no wintry weather chill him. No wind that blew was bitterer than he, no falling snow was more intent upon its purpose, no pelting rain less open to entreaty. Foul weather didn't know where to have him. The heaviest rain, and snow, and hail, and sleet, could boast of the advantage over him in only one respect. They often 'came down' handsomely, and Scrooge never did.

Nobody ever stopped him in the street to say, with gladsome looks, 'My dear Scrooge, how are you? When will you come to see me?' No beggars implored him to bestow a trifle, no children asked him what it was o'clock, no man or woman ever once in all his life inquired the way to such and such a place of Scrooge. Even the blind men's dogs appeared to know him; and when they saw him coming on, would tug their owners into doorways and up courts; and then would wag their tails as though they said, 'No eye at all is better than an evil eye, dark master!'

But what did Scrooge care!

Christmas Eve

Dickens begins his story on Christmas Eve, and shows Scrooge's unpleasant attitude to everyone with whom he comes into contact.

Once upon a time – of all the good days in the year, on Christmas Eve – old Scrooge sat busy in his counting-house. It was cold, bleak, biting weather: foggy withal: and he could hear the people in the court outside, go wheezing up and down, beating their hands upon their breasts and stamping their feet upon the pavement stones to warm them. The city clocks had only just gone three, but it was quite dark already – it had not been light all day – and candles were flaring in the windows of the neighbouring offices, like ruddy smears upon the palpable brown air. The fog came pouring in at every chink and keyhole, and was so dense without, that although the court was of the narrowest, the houses opposite were mere phantoms. To see the dingy cloud come drooping down, obscuring everything, one might have thought that Nature lived hard by, and was brewing on a large scale.

The door of Scrooge's counting-house was open that he might keep his eye upon his clerk, who in a dismal little cell beyond, a sort of tank, was copying letters. Scrooge had a very small fire, but the clerk's fire was so very much smaller that it looked like one coal. But he couldn't replenish it, for Scrooge kept the coalbox in his own room; and so surely as the clerk came in with the shovel, the master predicted that it would be necessary for them to part. Wherefore the clerk put on his white comforter, and tried to warm himself at the candle; in which effort, not being a man of a strong imagination, he failed.

'A merry Christmas, uncle! God save you!' cried a cheerful voice. It was the voice of Scrooge's nephew, who came upon him so quickly that this was the first intimation he had of his approach.

'Bah!' said Scrooge, 'Humbug!'

He had so heated himself with rapid walking in the fog and frost, this nephew of Scrooge's, that he was all in a glow; his face was ruddy and handsome; his eyes sparkled, and his breath smoked again.

'Christmas a humbug, uncle!' said Scrooge's nephew. 'You don't mean that, I am sure?'

'I do,' said Scrooge. 'Merry Christmas! What right have you to be merry? What reason have you to be merry? You're poor enough.'

'Come, then,' returned the nephew gaily. 'What right have you to be dismal? What reason have you to be morose? You're rich enough.'

Scrooge having no better answer ready on the spur of the moment, said, 'Bah!' again; and followed it up with 'Humbug.'

'Don't be cross, uncle!' said the nephew.

CONTINUED ☞

3 Devil's advocate (pairs)

Scrooge shows how little he cares about other people when he refuses to give money to two men who are collecting for charity. Dickens puts Scrooge's case against charity very strongly as a way of convincing the reader to feel the opposite.

When someone deliberately argues against an issue, as Dickens does here, we call this 'being a Devil's advocate' – literally, 'the Devil's defender'.

Dickens uses several techniques to make Scrooge's refusal to make a contribution seem wrong. Use a copy of the chart below to explore these techniques.

Episode	Technique	Example	Effect
Beginning	Focus on **vocabulary** to highlight Scrooge's feelings	'At the ominous word "liberality", Scrooge frowned ...'	This shows the reader that Scrooge thinks liberality is ...
Middle	Use of **questions** to lead an argument	Scrooge's questions: 'Are there no prisons?'	These show what Scrooge thinks should happen to ...
End	Use of **adjectives** (describing words)		
	Hyperbole (over-the-top expression)	When Scrooge says, 'if they would rather die ...'	

Christmas Eve (continued)

After his nephew leaves, two charity collectors come to his office to ask Scrooge for a donation.

'Scrooge and Marley's, I believe,' said one of the gentlemen, referring to his list. 'Have I the pleasure of addressing Mr Scrooge, or Mr Marley?'

'Mr Marley has been dead these seven years,' Scrooge replied. 'He died seven years ago, this very night.'

'We have no doubt his liberality is well represented by his surviving partner,' said the gentleman, presenting his credentials.

It certainly was; for they had been two kindred spirits. At the ominous word 'liberality', Scrooge frowned, and shook his head, and handed the credentials back.

'At this festive season of the year, Mr Scrooge,' said the gentleman, taking up a pen, 'it is more than usually desirable that we should make some slight provision for the Poor and destitute, who suffer greatly at the present time. Many thousands are in want of common necessaries; hundreds of thousands are in want of common comforts, sir.'

'Are there no prisons?' asked Scrooge.

'Plenty of prisons,' said the gentleman, laying down the pen again.

'And the Union workhouses?' demanded Scrooge. 'Are they still in operation?'

'They are. Still,' returned the gentleman, 'I wish I could say they were not.'

'The Treadmill and the Poor Law are in full vigour, then?'
said Scrooge.

'Both very busy, sir.'

'Oh! I was afraid, from what you said at first, that something had occurred to stop them in their useful course,' said Scrooge. 'I'm very glad to hear it.'

'Under the impression that they scarcely furnish Christian cheer of mind or body to the multitude,' returned the gentleman, 'a few of us are endeavouring to raise a fund to buy the Poor some meat and drink, and means of warmth. We choose this time because it is a time, of all others, when Want is keenly felt, and Abundance rejoices. What shall I put you down for?'

'Nothing!' Scrooge replied.

'You wish to be anonymous?'

'I wish to be left alone,' said Scrooge. 'Since you ask me what I wish, gentlemen, that is my answer. I don't make merry myself at Christmas and I can't afford to make idle people merry. I help to support the establishments I have mentioned – they cost enough; and those who are badly off must go there.'

'Many can't go there; and many would rather die.'

'If they would rather die,' said Scrooge, 'they had better do it, and decrease the surplus population.'

Linked Text

4 Is money evil? (small groups)

People often say that 'money is the root of all evil'. However, the original saying, which comes from the Bible, is 'the *love* of money is the root of all evil'. Discuss what these sayings mean and explain the difference between them. Which one do you think applies to Scrooge?

5 The dragon's teeth (pairs)

A. S. J. Tessimond uses *metaphors* to make money seem real, alive. Money is described as if it is behind everything unpleasant in life.

Work together to illustrate other metaphors in the poem.

I am the dragon's teeth which you have sown

The threat behind the smiling of the clock

I am the rustle of banknotes in your grave

6 Your own poetry (individual)

Draft a poem of your own using metaphor. You might write about a different subject, such as truth or love.

Money

The love of money is one of the main themes of A Christmas Carol. Here is a poem which takes the same theme.

I am your master and your master's master,
I am the dragon's teeth which you have sown
In the field of dead men's and of live men's bones.

I am the moving belt you cannot turn from
The threat behind the smiling of the clock:
The paper on which your days are signed and witnessed
Which only the mouse and the moth and the flame dare devour.
I am the rustle of banknotes in your graves,
The crackle of lawyers' seals beneath your tombstones,
Borne to the leaning ears of legatees.

I am the cunning one whose final cunning
Was to buy grace, to corner loveliness,
To make a bid for beauty and to win it
And lock it away.

A. S. J. Tessimond, 1902–1962

7 Horror (pairs)

It's dark. The two of you are spending the night in a creepy house. Imagine that one of you picks up a book and it turns into a toad, and when the other looks at a picture hanging on the wall it turns into a cat. What happens next? How do you express what you feel?

Either:
- Improvise a scene in which one of you believes in the strange apparitions and the other thinks it's imagination.

or
- Create a transformation like the one below.

8 Marley's face (pairs)

Read pages 15–17. Note down the strange thing that Scrooge sees and how he reacts. Use the chart below to structure your thoughts, then write a paragraph called 'Scrooge's Reaction'.

Disturbing phenomenon	Scrooge's reaction
The door-knocker which is turned into Marley's face	At first, he … Then, he …

9 Spot the tone (pairs)

Read the opening paragraph on the opposite page. Write notes on the tone of each sentence. For example, is it angry, definite, factual? What effect does Dickens achieve by varying his tone like this?

Haunting

Marley died seven years before the story begins. He was Scrooge's business partner and just as miserly. He is carrying long, heavy chains which make a frightening clanking noise.

Marley was dead, to begin with. There is no doubt whatever about that. The register of his burial was signed by the clergyman, the clerk, the undertaker, and the chief mourner. Scrooge signed it. And Scrooge's name was good upon the Stock Exchange for anything he chose to put his hand to.

Old Marley was as dead as a door-nail.

Scrooge knew he was dead? Of course he did. How could it be otherwise? Scrooge and he were partners for I don't know how many years. Scrooge was his sole executor, his sole administrator, his sole assign, his sole residuary legatee, his sole friend, and sole mourner.

Let any man explain to me, if he can, how it happened that Scrooge, having his key in the lock of the door, saw in the knocker, without its undergoing any intermediate process of change – not a knocker, but Marley's face.

Marley's face. It was not in impenetrable shadow as the other objects in the yard were, but it had a dismal light about it, like a bad lobster in a dark cellar. It was not angry or ferocious, but looked at Scrooge as Marley used to look: with ghostly spectacles turned up on its ghostly forehead. The hair was curiously stirred, as if by breath or hot air; and, though the eyes were wide open, they were perfectly motionless. That, and its livid colour, made it horrible; but its horror seemed to be in spite of the face and beyond its control, rather than a part of its own expression.

As Scrooge looked fixedly at this phenomenon, it was a knocker again.

To say that he was not startled, or that his blood was not conscious of a terrible sensation to which it had been a stranger from infancy, would be untrue. But he put his hand upon the key he had relinquished, turned it sturdily, walked in, and lighted his candle.

He *did* pause, with a moment's irresolution, before he shut the door; and he *did* look cautiously behind it first, as if he half expected to be terrified with the sight of Marley's pigtail sticking out into the hall. But there was nothing on the back of the door, except the screws and nuts that held the knocker on, so he said 'Pooh, pooh!' and closed it with a bang.

CONTINUED ☞

10 'I have sat invisible beside you' (pairs)

Read page 17. Then *either*:

- Note down all the details of the ghost's appearance. Create your own illustration of Marley's ghost.

or

- Write a poem called 'Jacob Marley's Ghost'. You could use Dickens' line, 'You are fettered. Tell me why' as a *refrain* (a repeated line) in your poem.

11 'That is no light part of my penance' (pairs)

Jacob Marley's ghost suffers. It's as though a list of tortures had been drawn up for him to live and relive.

- Copy and continue this column plan, which explores Jacob Marley's torments and the possible reasons for them.

Jacob Marley's torment	Reasons for choosing them
To be fettered with a heavy chain that clanks and must be dragged ...	It makes the victim aware of the weight of his crimes and ...

- Use your column plan to create a 'Torturer's Scroll' explaining Marley's torment and the reasons for it.

12 Prediction (individual)

Write down three things you think the spirits will tell Scrooge.

Haunting (continued)

But Scrooge was wrong to dismiss the idea of being haunted. Later on that evening, Marley's ghost warns Scrooge what will happen to him if he does not change his ways and says that he will send three spirits.

The spectre raised a cry, and shook its chain and wrung its shadowy hands.

'You are fettered,' said Scrooge, trembling. 'Tell me why.' 'I wear the chain I forged in life,' replied the Ghost. 'I made it link by link, and yard by yard; I girded it on of my own free will, and of my own free will I wore it. Is its pattern strange to *you*?'

Scrooge trembled more and more.

'Or would you know,' pursued the Ghost, 'the weight and length of the strong coil you bear yourself? It was full as heavy and as long as this, seven Christmas Eves ago. You have laboured on it since. It is a ponderous chain!'

Scrooge glanced about him on the floor, in the expectation of finding himself surrounded by some fifty or sixty fathoms of iron cable: but he could see nothing.

'Jacob,' he said, imploringly. 'Old Jacob Marley, tell me more. Speak comfort to me, Jacob!'

'I have none to give,' the Ghost replied. 'Hear me!' cried the Ghost. 'My time is nearly gone.'

'I will,' said Scrooge. 'But don't be hard upon me!'

'How it is that I appear before you in a shape that you can see, I may not tell. I have sat invisible beside you many and many a day.'

It was not an agreeable idea. Scrooge shivered, and wiped the perspiration from his brow.

'That is no light part of my penance,' pursued the Ghost. 'I am here tonight to warn you, that you have yet a chance and hope of escaping my fate.'

'You were always a good friend to me,' said Scrooge. 'Thank'ee!'

'You will be haunted,' resumed the Ghost, 'by Three Spirits.' Scrooge's countenance fell almost as low as the Ghost's had done.

'Is that the chance and hope you mentioned, Jacob?' he demanded, in a faltering voice.

'It is.'

'I – I think I'd rather not,' said Scrooge.

'Without their visits,' said the Ghost, 'you cannot hope to shun the path I tread. Expect the first tomorrow, when the bell tolls One.'

'Couldn't I take 'em all at once, and have it over, Jacob?' hinted Scrooge.

13 Regrets (groups of three)

Read the extract opposite and create three characters of your own. One of you has a regret, one has been ill-treated, and one is the ghost who tells what happened. Create your own drama. What was the turning point that changed everything?

Create an alternative version of events showing how the outcome could have been changed.

14 Language changes (pairs)

The Victorians spoke more formally than we do today. Look carefully at the conversation between Scrooge and Belle. What phrases would you use today? Why are they unfamiliar-sounding?

Find modern alternatives and present your new conversation to the class.

Create a column plan like the one started here, which analyses how language has changed.

Victorian phrase	Modern version	How the language has changed
'It matters little'	It doesn't matter much	The word-order has altered
'I am not changed'	I have not changed	The tense has changed from …

The Ghost of Christmas Past

The first spirit, the Ghost of Christmas Past, takes Scrooge back in time to when his fiancée, Belle, released him from their engagement because he loved money more than he loved her.

He was not alone, but sat by the side of a fair young girl in a mourning-dress: in whose eyes there were tears, which sparkled in the light that shone out of the Ghost of Christmas Past.

'It matters little,' she said, softly. 'To you, very little. Another idol has displaced me; and if it can cheer and comfort you in time to come, as I would have tried to do, I have no just cause to grieve.'

'What idol has displaced you?' he rejoined.

'A golden one.'

'What then?' he retorted. 'Even if I have grown so much wiser, what then? I am not changed towards you.'

She shook her head.

'Am I?'

'Our contract is an old one. It was made when we were both poor and content to be so, until, in good season, we could improve our worldly fortune by our patient industry. You *are* changed. When it was made, you were another man.'

'I was a boy,' he said impatiently.

'Your own feeling tells you that you were not what you are,' she returned. 'I am. That which promised happiness when we were one in heart, is fraught with misery now that we are two.'

'Have I ever sought release?'

'In words. No. Never. But if you were free today, tomorrow, yesterday, can even I believe that you would choose a dowerless girl? I release you. With a full heart, for the love of him you once were.'

He was about to speak; but with her head turned from him, she resumed. 'May you be happy in the life you have chosen!'

She left him, and they parted.

'Spirit!' said Scrooge, 'show me no more! Conduct me home. Why do you delight to torture me?'

15 Learning a lesson (pairs)

Read Dickens' description of Christmas at the Cratchits'. Scrooge is meant to learn a lesson by looking at a family enjoying themselves. Does Dickens have a lesson for us?

Write an essay using the spider diagram below which analyses what the ghost is trying to teach Scrooge, and how.

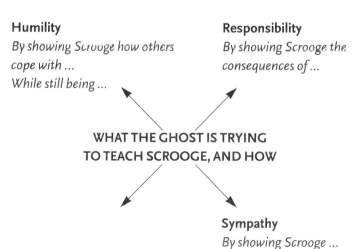

Humility
*By showing Scrooge how others
cope with ...
While still being ...*

Responsibility
*By showing Scrooge the
consequences of ...*

**WHAT THE GHOST IS TRYING
TO TEACH SCROOGE, AND HOW**

Sympathy
By showing Scrooge ...

Christmas at the Cratchits'

The second spirit, the Ghost of Christmas Present, shows Scrooge how his clerk, Bob Cratchit, and his family are celebrating Christmas in poverty.

'Whatever has got your precious father then?' said Mrs Cratchit. 'And your brother, Tiny Tim! And Martha warn't as late last Christmas Day by half-an-hour.'

'Here's Martha, mother!' said a girl, appearing as she spoke.

'Here's Martha, mother!' cried the two young Cratchits. 'Hurrah! There's *such* a goose, Martha!'

'Why, bless your heart alive, my dear, how late you are!' said Mrs Cratchit, kissing her a dozen times, and taking off her shawl and bonnet for her with officious zeal.

'We'd a deal of work to finish up last night,' replied the girl, 'and had to clear away this morning, mother!'

'Well! Never mind so long as you are come,' said Mrs Cratchit. 'Sit ye down before the fire, my dear, and have a warm, Lord bless ye!'

'No, no! There's father coming,' cried the two young Cratchits, who were everywhere at once. 'Hide, Martha, hide!'

So Martha hid herself, and in came little Bob, the father, with at least three feet of comforter exclusive of the fringe, hanging down before him; and his threadbare clothes darned up and brushed, to look seasonable; and Tiny Tim upon his shoulder. Alas for Tiny Tim; he bore a little crutch, and had his limbs supported by an iron frame!

'Why, where's our Martha?' cried Bob Cratchit, looking round.

'Not coming,' said Mrs Cratchit.

'Not coming!' said Bob, with a sudden declension in his high spirits; for he had been Tim's blood horse all the way from church, and had come home rampant. 'Not coming upon Christmas Day!'

Martha didn't like to see him disappointed, if it were only in joke; so she came out prematurely from behind the closet door, and ran into his arms, while the two young Cratchits hustled Tiny Tim, and bore him off into the wash-house, that he might hear the pudding singing in the copper.

'And how did little Tim behave?' asked Mrs Cratchit, when she had rallied Bob on his credulity, and Bob had hugged his daughter to his heart's content.

'As good as gold,' said Bob, 'and better. Somehow he gets thoughtful, sitting by himself so much, and thinks the strangest things you ever heard. He told me, coming home, that he hoped the people saw him in the church, because he was a cripple, and it might be pleasant to them to remember upon Christmas Day, who made lame beggars walk, and blind men see.'

Bob's voice was tremulous when he told them this, and trembled more when he said that Tiny Tim was growing strong and hearty.

Mrs Cratchit made the gravy (ready beforehand in a little saucepan) hissing hot; Master Peter mashed the potatoes with incredible vigour; Miss Belinda sweetened

CONTINUED ☞

Christmas at the Cratchits' (continued)

up the apple-sauce; Martha dusted the hot plates; Bob took Tiny Tim beside him in a tiny corner at the table; the two young Cratchits set chairs for everybody, not forgetting themselves, and mounting guard upon their posts, crammed spoons into their mouths, lest they should shriek for goose before their turn came to be helped. At last the dishes were set on, and grace was said. It was succeeded by a breathless pause, as Mrs Cratchit, looking slowly all along the carving-knife, prepared to plunge it in the breast; but when she did, and when the long expected gush of stuffing issued forth, one murmur of delight arose all round the board, and even Tiny Tim, excited by the two young Cratchits, beat on the table with the handle of his knife, and feebly cried 'Hurrah!'

There never was such a goose. Bob said he didn't believe there ever was such a goose cooked. Its tenderness and flavour, size and cheapness, were the themes of universal admiration. Eked out by apple-sauce and mashed potatoes, it was a sufficient dinner for the whole family; indeed, as Mrs Cratchit said with great delight (surveying one small atom of a bone upon the dish), they hadn't ate it all at last! Yet every one had had enough, and the youngest Cratchits in particular, were steeped in sage and onion to the eyebrows! But now, the plates being changed by Miss Belinda, Mrs Cratchit left the room alone – too nervous to bear witnesses – to take the pudding up and bring it in.

Hallo! A great deal of steam! The pudding was out of the copper. A smell like a washing-day! That was the cloth. A smell like an eating-house and a pastrycook's next door to each other, with a laundress's next door to that! That was the pudding! In half a minute Mrs Cratchit entered – flushed, but smiling proudly – with the pudding, like a speckled cannon-ball, so hard and firm, blazing in half of half-a-quartern of ignited brandy, and bedight with Christmas holly stuck into the top.

Oh, a wonderful pudding! Bob Cratchit said, and calmly too, that he regarded it as the greatest success achieved by Mrs Cratchit since their marriage. Mrs Cratchit said that now the weight was off her mind, she would confess she had had her doubts about the quantity of flour. Everybody had something to say about it, but nobody said or thought it was at all a small pudding for a large family. It would have been flat heresy to do so. Any Cratchit would have blushed to hint at such a thing.

At last the dinner was all done, the cloth was cleared, the hearth swept, and the fire made up. The compound in the jug being tasted, and considered perfect, apples and oranges were put upon the table, and a shovel-full of chestnuts on the fire. Then all the Cratchit family drew round the hearth, in what Bob Cratchit called a circle, meaning half a one; and at Bob Cratchit's elbow stood the family display of glass. Two tumblers, and a custard-cup without a handle.

These held the hot stuff from the jug, however, as well as golden goblets would have done; and Bob served it out with beaming looks, while the chestnuts on the fire sputtered and cracked noisily. Then Bob proposed:

'A Merry Christmas to us all, my dears. God bless us!'

Christmas at the Cratchits' (continued)

Which all the family re-echoed.

'God bless us every one!' said Tiny Tim, the last of all.

He sat very close to his father's side upon his little stool. Bob held his withered little hand in his, as if he loved the child, and wished to keep him by his side, and dreaded that he might be taken from him.

'Spirit,' said Scrooge, with an interest he had never felt before, 'tell me if Tiny Tim will live.'

'I see a vacant seat,' replied the Ghost, 'in the poor chimney-corner, and a crutch without an owner, carefully preserved. If these shadows remain unaltered by the Future, the child will die.'

'No, no,' said Scrooge. 'Oh, no, kind Spirit! Say he will be spared.'

'If these shadows remain unaltered by the Future, none other of my race', returned the Ghost, 'will find him here. What then? If he be like to die, he had better do it, and decrease the surplus population.'

Scrooge hung his head to hear his own words quoted by the Spirit, and was overcome with penitence and grief.

16 The technique of writing ghost stories (groups of three)

Writers of ghost stories try to frighten the reader by using certain techniques, and Dickens is no exception. Create a plan of the techniques Dickens uses in his ghost story by copying and completing this spider diagram.

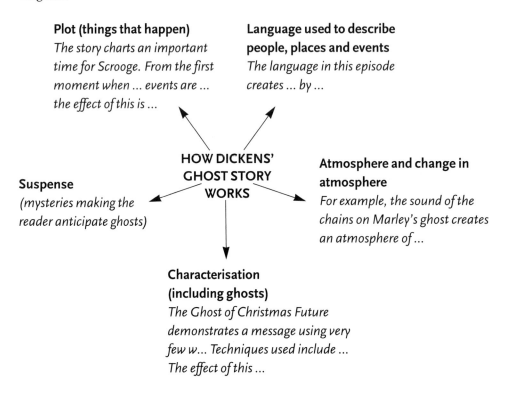

Plot (things that happen)
The story charts an important time for Scrooge. From the first moment when ... events are ... the effect of this is ...

Language used to describe people, places and events
The language in this episode creates ... by ...

HOW DICKENS' GHOST STORY WORKS

Suspense
(mysteries making the reader anticipate ghosts)

Atmosphere and change in atmosphere
For example, the sound of the chains on Marley's ghost creates an atmosphere of ...

Characterisation (including ghosts)
The Ghost of Christmas Future demonstrates a message using very few w... Techniques used include ... The effect of this ...

17 Scrooge sees his own grave (groups of four)

This moment is very important in Dickens' story. Imagine you are directing a film adaptation of this section of *A Christmas Carol*.

- Develop a storyboard with a clear script.
- Add notes on the techniques you would use to create tension.

The Ghost of Christmas Future

The third spirit, the Ghost of Christmas Future, shows Scrooge that he will die alone and unmourned if he continues with his present life-style.

'Spectre,' said Scrooge, 'something informs me that our parting moment is at hand. I know it, but I know not how. Tell me what man that was whom we saw lying dead?'

The Spirit stopped; the hand was pointed elsewhere.

He joined it once again, and wondering why and whither he had gone, accompanied it until they reached an iron gate. He paused to look round before entering.

A churchyard. Here, then, the wretched man whose name he had now to learn, lay underneath the ground. It was a worthy place. Walled in by houses; overrun by grass and weeds, the growth of vegetation's death, not life; choked up with too much burying; fat with repleted appetite. A worthy place!

The Spirit stood among the graves, and pointed down to One. He advanced towards it trembling. The Phantom was exactly as it had been, but he dreaded that he saw new meaning in its solemn shape.

'Before I draw nearer to that stone to which you point,' said Scrooge, 'answer me one question. Are these the shadows of the things that Will be, or are they shadows of things that May be, only?'

Still the Ghost pointed downward to the grave by which it stood.

Scrooge crept towards it, trembling as he went; and following the finger, read upon the stone of the neglected grave his own name, EBENEZER SCROOGE.

'Am *I* that man who lay upon the bed?' he cried, upon his knees.

The finger pointed from the grave to him, and back again.

'No, Spirit! Oh, no, no!'

The finger still was there.

'Spirit!' he cried, tight clutching at its robe, 'Hear me! Assure me that I yet may change these shadows you have shown me, by an altered life!'

The kind hand trembled.

'I will honour Christmas in my heart, and try to keep it all the year. I will live in the Past, the Present, and the Future. The Spirits of all Three shall strive within me. I will not shut out the lessons that they teach. Oh, tell me I may sponge away the writing on this stone!'

18 I changed my life: you can change yours (pairs)

Imagine Scrooge is going to appear on a television programme about people's lives. He is to be interviewed about how his life has changed. One of you takes the part of the interviewer, the other Scrooge. Use a copy of the chart below to plan your interview.

Interviewer: Characters and incidents I can ask questions about	Notes on Scrooge's thoughts about ...	Scrooge's thoughts after encountering the ghosts
Bob Marley	We were good friends once. I was just like him ...	I see that if I had carried on behaving like Bob Marley ...
Belle, Scrooge's fiancée		
Bob Cratchit		
The Cratchit family		
Whether Scrooge believes ...		

19 Does the title fit? (individual)

Why did Dickens call this story A Christmas Carol? Do you think it is a suitable story for Christmas? Explain your reasons.

Scrooge Reforms

Scrooge takes notice of the Spirits' message and the next day when he goes to work he is a changed man.

Scrooge was early at the office next morning. Oh, he was early there. If he could only be there first, and catch Bob Cratchit coming late! That was the thing he had set his heart upon.

And he did it; yes, he did! The clock struck nine. No Bob. A quarter past. No Bob. He was full eighteen minutes and a half behind his time. Scrooge sat with his door wide open, that he might see him come into the Tank.

His hat was off, before he opened the door; his comforter too. He was on his stool in a jiffy; driving away with his pen, as if he were trying to overtake nine o'clock. 'Hallo!' growled Scrooge, in his accustomed voice, as near as he could feign it. 'What do you mean by coming here at this time of day?'

'I am very sorry, sir,' said Bob, 'I *am* behind my time.'

'You are?' repeated Scrooge. 'Yes. I think you are. Step this way, sir, if you please.'

'It's only once a year, sir,' pleaded Bob, appearing from the Tank. 'It shall not be repeated. I was making rather merry yesterday, sir.'

'Now, I'll tell you what, my friend,' said Scrooge, 'I am not going to stand this sort of thing any longer. And therefore,' he continued, leaping from his stool, and giving Bob such a dig in the waistcoat that he staggered back into the Tank again; 'and therefore I am about to raise your salary!'

Bob trembled, and got a little nearer to the ruler. He had a momentary idea of knocking Scrooge down with it, holding him, and calling to the people in the court for help and a strait-waistcoat.

'A merry Christmas, Bob!' said Scrooge, with an earnestness that could not be mistaken, as he clapped him on the back. 'A merrier Christmas, Bob, my good fellow, than I have given you, for many a year! I'll raise your salary, and endeavour to assist your struggling family, and we will discuss your affairs this very afternoon, over a Christmas bowl of smoking bishop, Bob! Make up the fires, and buy another coal-scuttle before you dot another i, Bob Cratchit!'

Scrooge was better than his word. He did it all, and infinitely more; and to Tiny Tim, who did *not* die, he was a second father.

OLIVER TWIST

An Orphan's Adventures

1 Wild, hungry eyes (groups of five)

The boys in the workhouse are starving and Oliver is the one who has to go
and ask for more food. After reading the extract opposite, imagine you are a
group of orphans in a workhouse.

Act out the scene opposite, taking parts as the master, the boy from the
cookshop, Oliver and the other orphans. You will need to plan dialogue,
movement and timing.

2 Ward of the parish (individual)

How did Oliver feel when he saw this poster? What were his hopes for the
future?

Write a diary entry expressing Oliver's feelings.

Oliver Asks for More

Oliver's mother died giving birth to him. After being fostered he was sent to the workhouse when he was considered old enough to earn his own living. He was nine years old.

The bowls never wanted washing. The boys polished them with their spoons till they shone again. Boys have generally excellent appetites. Oliver Twist and his companions suffered the tortures of slow starvation for three months: at last they got so voracious and wild with hunger that one boy, who was tall for his age, and hadn't been used to that sort of thing (for his father had kept a small cookshop), hinted darkly to his companions, that unless he had another basin of gruel every day, he was afraid he might some night happen to eat the boy who slept next him, who happened to be a weakly youth of tender age. He had a wild, hungry eye; and they implicitly believed him. A council was held; lots were cast who should walk up to the master after supper that evening, and ask for more; and it fell to Oliver Twist.

The evening arrived; the boys took their places. The master, in his cook's uniform, stationed himself at the copper; his pauper assistants ranged themselves behind him; the gruel was served out; and a long grace was said over the short commons. The gruel disappeared; the boys whispered each other, and winked at Oliver, while his next neighbours nudged him. Child as he was, he was desperate with hunger and reckless with misery. He rose from the table, and advancing to the master, basin and spoon in hand, said: somewhat alarmed at his own temerity:

'Please, sir, I want some more.'

The master was a fat, healthy man; but he turned very pale. He gazed in stupefied astonishment on the small rebel for some seconds, and then clung for support to the copper. The assistants were paralysed with wonder; the boys with fear.

'What!' said the master at length, in a faint voice.

'Please, sir,' replied Oliver, 'I want some more.'

The master aimed a blow at Oliver's head with the ladle, pinioned him in his arms, and shrieked aloud for the beadle.*

Oliver was ordered into instant confinement; and a bill was next morning pasted on the outside of the gate, offering a reward of five pounds to anybody who would take Oliver Twist off the hands of the parish. In other words, five pounds and Oliver Twist were offered to any man or woman who wanted an apprentice to any trade, business, or calling.

* The beadle was in charge of discipline.

3 Getting to know Oliver (pairs)

Dickens gives us a great deal of information about Oliver at this early stage in the story. Use the diagram below to gather evidence about Oliver's character.

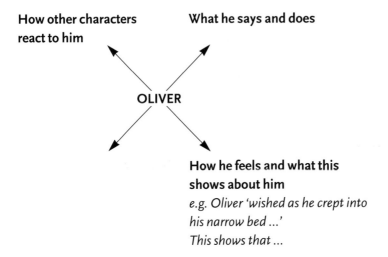

How other characters react to him

What he says and does

OLIVER

How he feels and what this shows about him
e.g. Oliver 'wished as he crept into his narrow bed ...'
This shows that ...

4 Amongst the coffins (pairs)

Oliver is left alone at night surrounded by coffins. Imagine how he feels. Make notes about what he can see, hear, touch and imagine.

Use your notes to draft a poem or descriptive passage written as Oliver (in the first person), called 'I am amongst the coffins'.

5 Manipulating the reader (pairs)

Writers choose their words with great care to get a response from their readers. How are Dickens' words chosen to make readers sympathise with Oliver? Consider the following points and feed back to the class.

- What is the effect of Oliver's employers' name 'Sowerberry' ?
- What *adjectives* (describing words) are used about Mrs Sowerberry?
- How is *repetition* (of words or phrases) used to create effect?
- What *verb* (doing word) tells how Oliver is put into the 'stone cell'?

The Undertaker's Apprentice

Mr Gamfield, the chimney sweep, answers the advertisement which offered five pounds to take Oliver as an apprentice.

'This here boy, sir, wot the parish wants to 'prentis,' said Mr Gamfield.

'Ay, my man,' said the gentleman in the white waistcoat, with a condescending smile. 'What of him?'

'If the parish vould like him to learn a right pleasant trade, in a good 'spectable chimbley-sweepin' bisness,' said Mr Gamfield, 'I wants a 'prentis, and I am ready to take him.'

'Walk in,' said the gentleman in the white waistcoat.

'It's a nasty trade,' said Mr Limbkins.

'Young boys have been smothered in chimneys before now,' said another gentleman.

'That's acause they damped the straw afore they lit it in the chimbley to make 'em come down agin,' said Gamfield; 'that's all smoke, and no blaze; vereas smoke ain't o' no use at all in making a boy come down, for it only sinds him to sleep, and that's wot he likes. Boys is wery obstinit, and wery lazy, gen'lmen, and there's nothink like a good hot blaze to make 'em come down vith a run. It's humane too, gen'lmen, acause, even if they've stuck in the chimbley, roasting their feet makes 'em struggle to hextricate theirselves.'

The gentleman in the white waistcoat appeared very much amused by this explanation; but his mirth was speedily checked by a look from Mr Limbkins. The board then proceeded to converse among themselves for a few minutes.

At length the whispering ceased; and the members of the board, having resumed their seats and their solemnity, Mr Limbkins said:

'We have considered your proposition, and we don't approve of it.'

'Not at all,' said the gentleman in the white waistcoat.

'Decidedly not,' added the other members.

As Mr Gamfield did happen to labour under the slight imputation of having bruised three or four boys to death already, it occurred to him that the board had, perhaps, taken it into their heads that this extraneous circumstance ought to influence their proceedings. He twisted his cap in his hands, and walked slowly from the table.

The undertaker, who had just put up the shutters of his shop, was making some entries in his day-book by the light of a most appropriately dismal candle, when Mr Bumble entered.

'Aha!', said the undertaker, looking up from the book, and pausing in the middle of a word; 'is that you, Bumble?'

'No one else, Mr Sowerberry,' replied the beadle. 'Here! I've brought the boy.' Oliver made a bow.

'Oh! that's the boy, is it?' said the undertaker, raising the candle above his head, to

CONTINUED ☞

The Undertaker's Apprentice (continued)

get a better view of Oliver. 'Mrs Sowerberry, will you have the goodness to come here a moment, my dear?'

Mrs Sowerberry emerged from a little room behind the shop, and presented the form of a short, thin, squeezed-up woman, with a vixenish countenance.

'My dear,' said Mr Sowerberry, deferentially, 'this is the boy from the workhouse that I told you of.' Oliver bowed again.

'Dear me!' said the undertaker's wife, 'he's very small.'

'Why, he *is* rather small,' replied Mr Bumble, looking at Oliver as if it were his fault that he was no bigger; 'he *is* small. There's no denying it. But he'll grow, Mrs Sowerberry – he'll grow.'

'Ah! I dare say he will,' replied the lady pettishly, 'on our victuals and our drink. I see no saving in parish children, not I; for they always cost more to keep, than they're worth. However, men always think they know best. There! Get down stairs, little bag o' bones.' With this, the undertaker's wife opened a side door, and pushed Oliver down a steep flight of stairs into a stone cell, damp and dark, forming the ante-room of the coal-cellar, and denominated 'kitchen', wherein sat a slatternly girl, in shoes down at heel, and blue worsted stockings very much out of repair.

'Here, Charlotte,' said Mrs Sowerberry, who had followed Oliver down, 'give this boy some of the cold bits that were put by for Trip. He hasn't come home since the morning, so he may go without 'em. I dare say the boy isn't too dainty to eat 'em, – are you, boy?'

Oliver, whose eyes had glistened at the mention of meat, and who was trembling with eagerness to devour it, replied in the negative; and a plateful of coarse broken victuals was set before him.

I wish some well-fed philosopher, whose meat and drink turn to gall within him; whose blood is ice, whose heart is iron; could have seen Oliver Twist clutching at the dainty viands that the dog had neglected. I wish he could have witnessed the horrible avidity with which Oliver tore the bits asunder with all the ferocity of famine. There is only one thing I should like better; and that would be to see the Philosopher making the same sort of meal himself, with the same relish.

'Well,' said the undertaker's wife, when Oliver had finished his supper: which she had regarded in silent horror, and with fearful auguries of his future appetite: 'have you done?'

There being nothing eatable within his reach, Oliver replied in the affirmative.

'Then come with me,' said Mrs Sowerberry, taking up a dim and dirty lamp, and leading the way upstairs; 'your bed's under the counter. You don't mind sleeping among the coffins, I suppose? But it doesn't much matter whether you do or don't, for you can't sleep anywhere else. Come; don't keep me here all night!'

Oliver lingered no longer, but meekly followed his new mistress.

Oliver, being left to himself in the undertaker's shop, set the lamp down on a workman's bench, and gazed timidly about him with a feeling of awe and dread,

The Undertaker's Apprentice (continued)

which many people a good deal older than he, will be at no loss to understand. An unfinished coffin on black tressels, which stood in the middle of the shop, looked so gloomy and death-like that a cold tremble came over him, every time his eyes wandered in the direction of the dismal object, from which he almost expected to see some frightful form slowly rear its head, to drive him mad with terror. Against the wall were ranged, in regular array, a long row of elm boards cut into the same shape: looking in the dim light, like high-shouldered ghosts with their hands in their breeches-pockets. Coffin-plates, elm-chips, bright-headed nails, and shreds of black cloth, lay scattered on the floor; and the wall behind the counter was ornamented with a lively representation of two mutes in very stiff neckcloths, on duty at a large private door, with a hearse drawn by four black steeds, approaching in the distance. The shop was close and hot. The atmosphere seemed tainted with the smell of coffins. The recess beneath the counter in which his flock mattress was thrust looked like a grave.

Nor were these the only dismal feelings which depressed Oliver. He was alone in a strange place; and we all know how chilled and desolate the best of us will sometimes feel in such a situation. The boy had no friends to care for, or to care for him. The regret of no recent separation was fresh in his mind; the absence of no loved and well-remembered face sank heavily into his heart. But his heart *was* heavy, notwithstanding; and he wished, as he crept into his narrow bed, that that were his coffin, and that he could be lain in a calm and lasting sleep in the churchyard ground, with the tall grass waving gently above his head, and the sound of the old deep bell to soothe him in his sleep.

6 A new classmate (pairs)

A new pupil has joined the class and feels shy. A confident pupil offers to show him or her around. Improvise the scene.

7 Language work (pairs)

The Artful Dodger speaks in a cockney dialect. List the words he uses, in a table like this and find modern alternatives.

The Artful Dodger's words	What they mean	What we say today
'Hullo, my covey!'	A greeting	'Hello mate.'
'What's the row?'	What's the matter?	'What's up?'
'grub'		
'at low-water mark'		

What impression does the Artful Dodger's language create?

The Artful Dodger

Oliver runs away from the Sowerberrys' to London. It takes him seven days to walk there, and he is soon befriended by the Artful Dodger.

'Hullo, my covey! What's the row?'

The boy who addressed this inquiry to the young wayfarer, was about his own age, but one of the queerest-looking boys that Oliver had ever seen. He was a snub-nosed, flat-browed, common-faced boy enough; and as dirty a juvenile as one would wish to see; but he had about him all the airs and manners of a man. His hat was stuck on the top of his head so lightly, that it threatened to fall off every moment.

He wore a man's coat, which reached nearly to his heels. He had turned the cuffs back, half-way up his arm, to get his hands out of the sleeves: apparently with the ultimate view of thrusting them into the pockets of his corduroy trousers; for there he kept them.

'I am very hungry and tired,' replied Oliver, the tears standing in his eyes as he spoke. 'I have walked a long way. I have been walking these seven days.'

'Walking for sivin days! Come,' said the young gentleman; 'you want grub, and you shall have it. I'm at low-water mark myself – only one bob and a magpie, but, as far as it goes, I'll fork out and stump. Up with you on your pins. There! Now then!'

Assisting Oliver to rise, the young gentleman took him to an adjacent chandler's shop, where he purchased a sufficiency of ready-dressed ham and a half-quartern loaf, or, as he himself expressed it, 'a fourpenny bran!' the ham being kept clean and preserved from dust, by the ingenious expedient of making a hole in the loaf by pulling out a portion of the crumb, and stuffing it therein. Taking the bread under his arm, the young gentleman turned into a small public-house, and led the way to a tap-room in the rear of the premises. Here, a pot of beer was brought in, by direction of the mysterious youth; and Oliver, falling to, at his new friend's bidding, made a long and hearty meal, during the progress of which, the strange boy eyed him from time to time with great attention.

'Going to London?' said the strange boy, when Oliver had at length concluded.

'Yes.'

'Got any lodgings?'

'No.'

'Money?'

'No.'

The strange boy whistled; and put his arms into his pockets, as far as the big coat-sleeves would let them go.

'Do you live in London?' inquired Oliver.

'Yes. I do, when I'm at home,' replied the boy. 'I suppose you want some place to sleep in tonight, don't you?'

8 Games (group discussion)

What party or playground games can you remember? Describe the rules
and discuss the skills they involve. Use the chart below as a beginning.

Name of game	Rules	Skill that is involved
Blind Man's Buff	Blindfolded person has to catch and identify someone from a group	Moving in silence, listening carefully
Conkers		Precision swings

9 The merry old gentleman (pairs)

The Artful Dodger takes Oliver home to meet Fagin. Oliver doesn't realise
that Fagin is training the group of boys to steal; he thinks they are playing 'a
very curious and uncommon game'. The reader, though, can see that Fagin
is training the boys to steal. There is, then, a double meaning in this
passage, which is called called *irony*. When you can read two meanings in a
passage, the writer is using the technique known as irony.
Either:
Plan and draft an ironic passage, involving an innocent like Oliver who does
not understand the significance of a series of events.
Or:
Draw your own illustration for the text on page 37. Underneath, write a
caption which explains the irony of the game.

The School for Thieves

The Artful Dodger takes Oliver to where he lives with Fagin, who is training a group of young boys to become thieves.

When the breakfast was cleared away, the merry old gentleman and the two boys played at a very curious and uncommon game, which was performed in this way. The merry old gentleman, placing a snuff-box in one pocket of his trousers, a note-case in the other, and a watch in his waistcoat pocket, with a guard-chain round his neck, and sticking a mock diamond pin in his shirt: buttoned his coat tight round him, and putting his spectacle-case and handkerchief in his pockets, trotted up and down the room with a stick, in imitation of the manner in which old gentlemen walk about the streets any hour in the day. Sometimes he stopped at the fireplace and sometimes at the door, making believe that he was staring with all his might into shop-windows. At such times he would look constantly round him, for fear of thieves, and would keep slapping all his pockets in turn, to see that he hadn't lost anything, in such a very funny and natural manner, that Oliver laughed till the tears ran down his face. All this time, the two boys followed him closely about, getting out of his sight, so nimbly, every time he turned round, that it was impossible to follow their motions. At last, the Dodger trod upon his toes, or ran upon his boot accidentally, while Charley Bates stumbled up against him behind; and in that one moment they took from him, with the most extraordinary rapidity, snuff-box, note-case, watch-guard, chain, shirt-pin, pocket-handkerchief – even the spectacle-case. If the old gentleman felt a hand in any one of his pockets, he cried out where it was; and then the game began all over again.

'Is my handkerchief hanging out of my pocket, my dear?' said the Jew, stopping short.

'Yes, sir,' said Oliver.

'See if you can take it out, without my feeling it.'

Oliver held up the bottom of the pocket with one hand, as he had seen the Dodger hold it, and drew the handkerchief lightly out of it with the other.

'Is it gone?' cried the Jew.

'Here it is, sir,' said Oliver, showing it in his hand.

'You're a clever boy, my dear,' said the playful old gentleman, patting Oliver on the head approvingly. 'I never saw a sharper lad. Here's a shilling for you. If you go on, in this way, you'll be the greatest man of the time.'

10 Another world (groups of three)

When Oliver is caught stealing and rescued by Mr Brownlow, he sees
another way of living. Note down all the new things he encounters, and
describe his reaction to them.

11 Mr Brownlow (pairs)

Imagine a meeting in a coffee-house between Mr Brownlow and one of his
friends. Act out a scene where they discuss how he rescued Oliver, and talk
about what Mr Brownlow should do next. Why might the friend doubt
Oliver's honesty?

12 A time of calm (pairs)

Writers vary their technique to create atmosphere. This passage shows
Oliver in a happy and calm moment of his life. Use a chart like this to
explore the techniques Dickens uses to create this atmosphere.

Technique	Evidence	Example
Sentence structure and length	Varied use of long complex sentences and shorter simple ones. The effect of this is …	
Content of dialogue	Conversation is thoughtful, dealing with ideas not actions. The effect of this is …	
Contrast between past and present		

Mr Brownlow's World

Fagin takes Oliver out on the streets where he sees the Artful Dodger picking pockets and finally understands the truth about the 'game'. The alarm is raised and Oliver is caught, but he is rescued from prison by a kindly gentleman, Mr Brownlow, who takes him home and cares for him. Oliver is ill for some time.

They were happy days, those of Oliver's recovery. Everything was so quiet, and neat, and orderly; everybody was kind and gentle; that after the noise and turbulence in the midst of which he had always lived, it seemed like Heaven itself. He was no sooner strong enough to put his clothes on, properly, than Mr Brownlow caused a complete new suit, and a new cap, and a new pair of shoes, to be provided for him. Oliver tapped at the study door. On Mr Brownlow calling to him to come in, he found himself in a little back room, quite full of books, with a window, looking into some pleasant little gardens. There was a table drawn up before the window, at which Mr Brownlow was seated reading. When he saw Oliver, he pushed the book away from him, and told him to come near the table, and sit down. Oliver complied; marvelling where the people could be found to read such a great number of books as seemed to be written to make the world wiser. Which is still a marvel to more experienced people than Oliver Twist, every day of their lives.

'There are a good many books, are there not, my boy?' said Mr Brownlow, observing the curiosity with which Oliver surveyed the shelves that reached from the floor to the ceiling.

'A great number, sir,' replied Oliver. 'I never saw so many.'

'You shall read them, if you behave well,' said the old gentleman kindly. 'How should you like to grow up a clever man, and write books, eh?'

'I think I would rather read them, sir,' replied Oliver.

'What! Wouldn't you like to be a book-writer?' said the old gentleman.

Oliver considered a little while; and at last said, he should think it would be a much better thing to be a bookseller; upon which the old gentleman laughed heartily, and declared he had said a very good thing. Which Oliver felt glad to have done, though he by no means knew what it was.

'Well, well,' said the old gentleman, composing his features. 'Don't be afraid! We won't make an author of you, while there's an honest trade to be learnt, or brickmaking to turn to.'

'Thank you, sir,' said Oliver. At the earnest manner of his reply, the old gentleman laughed again.

'Now,' said Mr Brownlow, speaking if possible in a kinder, but at the same time in a much more serious manner, than Oliver had ever known him assume yet, 'I want you to pay great attention, my boy, to what I am going to say.'

'Oh, don't tell me you are going to send me away, sir, pray!' exclaimed Oliver, alarmed at the serious tone of the old gentleman's commencement! 'Don't turn me out of doors to wander in the streets again. Let me stay here, and be a servant. Don't send me back to the wretched place I came from. Have mercy upon a poor boy, sir!'

13 Film proposal (pairs)

Imagine a film company has asked you to submit a proposal for the scene where Oliver has been recaptured and taken back to Fagin's den.

Your proposal should include:
- a detailed storyboard of at least four frames with guidance for set, special effects (like music or lights) and dialogue
- casting suggestions.

Here are some ideas:

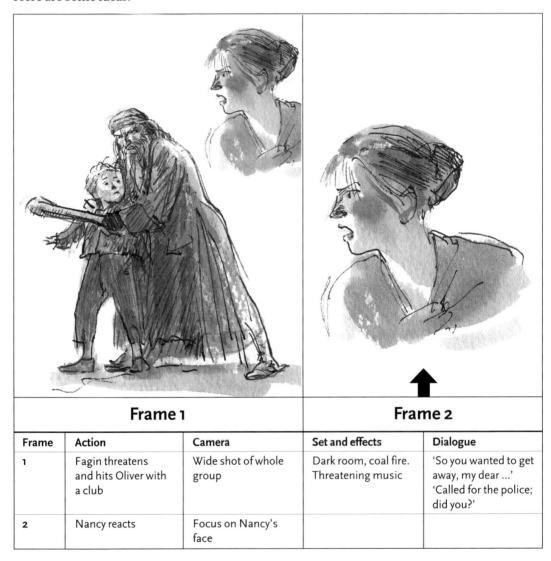

Frame 1			Frame 2	

Frame	Action	Camera	Set and effects	Dialogue
1	Fagin threatens and hits Oliver with a club	Wide shot of whole group	Dark room, coal fire. Threatening music	'So you wanted to get away, my dear ...' 'Called for the police; did you?'
2	Nancy reacts	Focus on Nancy's face		

Nancy Protects Oliver

Oliver settles down well to life with Mr Brownlow. But one day, when he is out of the house on an errand, he is kidnapped by Nancy and Bill Sikes, adult members of Fagin's gang. They return him to Fagin.

'So you wanted to get away, my dear, did you?' said the Jew, taking up a jagged and knotted club which lay in a corner of the fireplace; 'eh?'

Oliver made no reply. But he watched the Jew's motions, and breathed quickly.

'Wanted to get assistance; called for the police; did you?' sneered the Jew, catching the boy by the arm. 'We'll cure you of that, my young master.'

The Jew inflicted a smart blow on Oliver's shoulders with the club; and was raising it for a second, when the girl, rushing forward, wrested it from his hand. She flung it into the fire, with a force that brought some of the glowing coals whirling out into the room.

'I won't stand by and see it done, Fagin,' cried the girl. 'You've got the boy, and what more would you have? – Let him be – let him be – or I shall put that mark on some of you, that will bring me to the gallows before my time.'

The girl stamped her foot violently on the floor as she vented this threat; and with her lips compressed, and her hands clenched, looked alternately at the Jew and the other robber: her face quite colourless from the passion of rage into which she had gradually worked herself.

'I thieved for you when I was a child not half as old as this!' pointing to Oliver. 'I have been in the same trade, and in the same service, for twelve years since. Don't you know it? Speak out! Don't you know it?'

'Well, well,' replied the Jew, with an attempt at pacification; 'and if you have, it's your living!'

'Aye, it is!' returned the girl; not speaking, but pouring out the words in one continuous and vehement scream. 'It is my living; and the cold, wet, dirty streets are my home; and you're the wretch that drove me to them long ago, and that'll keep me there, day and night, day and night, till I die!'

'I shall do you a mischief!' interposed the Jew, goaded by these reproaches; 'a mischief worse than that, if you say much more!'

The girl said nothing more; but, tearing her hair and dress in a transport of passion, made such a rush at the Jew as would probably have left signal marks of her revenge upon him, had not her wrists been seized by Sikes at the right moment; upon which, she made a few ineffectual struggles, and fainted.

'She's all right now,' said Sikes, laying her down in a corner. 'She's uncommon strong in the arms when she's up in this way.'

The Jew wiped his forehead, and smiled, as if it were a relief to have the disturbance over; but neither he, nor Sikes, nor the dog, nor the boys, seemed to consider it in any other light than a common occurrence incidental to business.

'It's the worst of having to do with women,' said the Jew, replacing his club; 'but they're clever, and we can't get on, in our line, without 'em. Charley, show Oliver to bed.'

14 Do it! (pairs)

Imagine one of you is trying to force the other to do something against his or her will: for example, walk the dog in the rain or play sport in the cold.

Improvise a scene in which one of you uses only verbal persuasion to influence the other.

15 A well-planned operation (groups of three)

Read pages 43–45 and note down the evidence showing that Toby Crackit knows the house well.

Discuss how he might have planned this operation. Why did it go so wrong?

16 A time of terror (pairs)

Dickens changes the atmosphere in this scene to one of fear and terror. What techniques does he use to create this?

Consider:
- sentence length
- exclamation (a short spoken dramatic sentence: 'Hush!')
- direct speech (the words actually spoken by a character: 'The boy next,' said Toby)

Look back to Activity 12 on page 38 for help with this.

The Burglary

Oliver is locked up by the gang for some weeks, then Bill Sikes and Toby Cruckit take him to burgle a remote mansion outside London. Oliver is useful because he is small enough to get through a window. Bill has threatened to murder Oliver if he makes a mess of the job.

After walking about a quarter of a mile, they stopped before a detached house surrounded by a wall: to the top of which, Toby Crackit, scarcely pausing to take breath, climbed in a twinkling.

'The boy next,' said Toby. 'Hoist him up; I'll catch hold of him.' Before Oliver had time to look round, Sikes had caught him under the arms; and in three or four seconds he and Toby were lying on the grass on the other side. Sikes followed directly. And they stole cautiously towards the house.

And now, for the first time, Oliver, well-nigh mad with grief and terror, saw that housebreaking and robbery, if not murder, were the objects of the expedition. He clasped his hands together, and involuntarily uttered a subdued exclamation of horror. A mist came before his eyes; the cold sweat stood upon his ashy face; his limbs failed him; and he sank upon his knees.

'Get up!' murmured Sikes, trembling with rage, and drawing the pistol from his pocket; 'Get up, or I'll strew your brains upon the grass.'

'Oh! for God's sake let me go!' cried Oliver; 'let me run away and die in the fields. I will never come near London; never, never! Oh! pray have mercy on me, and do not make me steal. For the love of all the bright Angels that rest in Heaven, have mercy upon me!'

The man to whom this appeal was made, swore a dreadful oath, and had cocked the pistol, when Toby, striking it from his grasp, placed his hand upon the boy's mouth, and dragged him to the house.

'Hush!' cried the man; 'it won't answer here. Say another word, and I'll do your business myself with a crack on the head. That makes no noise, and is quite as certain, and more genteel. Here, Bill, wrench the shutter open. He's game enough now, I'll engage. I've seen older hands of his age took the same way, for a minute or two, on a cold night.'

Sikes, invoking terrific imprecations upon Fagin's head for sending Oliver on such an errand, plied the crowbar vigorously, but with little noise. After some delay, and some assistance from Toby, the shutter to which he had referred, swung open on its hinges.

It was a little lattice window, about five feet and a half above the ground, at the back of the house: which belonged to a scullery, or small brewing-place, at the end of the passage. The aperture was so small, that the inmates had probably not thought it worth while to defend it more securely; but it was large enough to admit a boy of Oliver's size, nevertheless. A very brief exercise of Mr Sikes's art sufficed to overcome the fastening of the lattice; and it soon stood wide open also.

CONTINUED ☞

The Burglary (continued)

'Now listen, you young limb,' whispered Sikes, drawing a dark lantern from his pocket, and throwing the glare full on Oliver's face; 'I'm going to put you through there. Take this light; go softly up the steps straight afore you, and along the little hall, to the street-door; unfasten it, and let us in.'

'There's a bolt at the top, you won't be able to reach,' interposed Toby. 'Stand upon one of the hall chairs. There are three there, Bill, with a jolly large blue unicorn and gold pitchfork on 'em; which is the old lady's arms.'

'Keep quiet, can't you?' replied Sikes, with a threatening look. 'The room-door is open, is it?'

'Wide,' replied Toby, after peeping in to satisfy himself. 'The game of that is, that they always leave it open with a catch, so that the dog, who's got a bed in here, may walk up and down the passage when he feels wakeful. Ha! ha! Barney 'ticed him away tonight. So neat!'

Although Mr Crackit spoke in a scarcely audible whisper, and laughed without noise, Sikes imperiously commanded him to be silent, and to get to work. Toby complied, by first producing his lantern, and placing it on the ground; then by planting himself firmly with his head against the wall beneath the window, and his hands upon his knees, so as to make a step of his back. This was no sooner done, than Sikes, mounting upon him, put Oliver gently through the window with his feet first; and, without leaving hold of his collar, planted him safely on the floor inside.

'Take this lantern,' said Sikes, looking into the room. 'You see the stairs afore you?'

Oliver, more dead than alive, gasped out 'Yes.' Sikes, pointing to the street-door with the pistol-barrel, briefly advised him to take notice that he was within shot all the way; and that if he faltered, he would fall dead that instant.

'It's done in a minute,' said Sikes, in the same low whisper. 'Directly I leave go of you, do your work. Hark!'

'What's that?' whispered the other man.

They listened intently.

'Nothing,' said Sikes, releasing his hold of Oliver. 'Now!'

In the short time he had had to collect his senses, the boy had firmly resolved that, whether he died in the attempt or not, he would make one effort to dart up stairs from the hall, and alarm the family. Filled with this idea, he advanced at once, but stealthily.

'Come back!' suddenly cried Sikes aloud. 'Back! back!'

Scared by the sudden breaking of the dead stillness of the place, and by a loud cry which followed it, Oliver let his lantern fall, knew not whether to advance or fly.

The cry was repeated – a light appeared – a vision of two terrified, half-dressed men at the top of the stairs swam before his eyes – a flash – a loud noise – a smoke – a crash somewhere, but where he knew not, – and he staggered back.

The Burglary (continued)

Sikes had disappeared for an instant, but he was up again, and had him by the collar before the smoke had cleared away. He fired his own pistol after the men, who were already retreating; and dragged the boy up.

'Clasp your arm tighter,' said Sikes, as he drew him through the window. 'Give me a shawl here. They've hit him. Quick! Damnation. how the boy bleeds!'

Then came the loud ringing of a bell, mingled with the noise of fire-arms. and the shouts of men, and the sensation of being carried over uneven ground at a rapid pace. And then, the noises grew confused in the distance; and a cold deadly feeling crept over the boy's heart; and he saw or heard no more.

Linked Text

17 The sentence of the law was fulfilled (pairs)

At the beginning of the nineteenth century it was common for criminals to be publicly hanged. Sir Walter Scott describes a public execution in the novel *The Heart of Midlothian*.

Discuss Sir Walter Scott's portrayal of the execution, answering the following questions:

- How was the process of Wilson's execution different from those of a later date?
- What extra precautions were taken to prevent him escaping?
- What should prisoners be meditating about as they go to their execution?

18 Phrasebook (individual)

Write a Victorian phrasebook explaining difficult vocabulary in this text. Organise the words in alphabetical order and explain whether they are *verbs* (doing words), *nouns* (naming words), *adjectives* (words describing nouns) or *adverbs* (words modifying verbs).

Word	Part of speech	Meaning
to be manacled	verb	to be handcuffed
scaffold		

19 Metaphor (pairs)

'The space that divided time from eternity'.

Sir Walter Scott uses this *metaphor* (describing one thing in terms of another) at a key moment in the passage. What does this metaphor mean?

The Heart of Midlothian

It was the custom, until within these thirty years, or thereabouts, to use the Grassmarket in Edinburgh for the scene of public executions. The fatal day was announced to the public by the appearance of a huge black gallows-tree towards the eastern end. This ill-omened apparition was of great height, with a scaffold surrounding it, and a double ladder placed against it, for the ascent of the unhappy criminal and the executioner. As this apparatus was always arranged before dawn, it seemed as if the gallows had grown out of the earth in the course of one night, like the production of some foul demon; and I well remember the fright with which the schoolboys, when I was one of their number, used to regard these ominous signs of deadly preparation. This mode of execution is now exchanged for one similar to that in front of Newgate – with what beneficial effect is uncertain. The mental sufferings of the convict are indeed shortened. He no longer stalks between the attendant clergymen, dressed in his grave-clothes, through a considerable part of the city, looking like a moving and walking corpse, while yet an inhabitant of this world.

On the 7th day of September, 1736, these ominous preparations for execution were made in the place we have described; and at an early hour the space around began to be occupied by several groups, who gazed on the scaffold and gibbet with a stern and vindictive show of satisfaction. When Wilson, the unhappy criminal, was delivered to Porteous by the keeper of the prison, in order that he might be conducted to the place of execution, Porteous, not satisfied with the usual precautions to prevent escape, ordered him to be manacled. This might be justifiable from the character and bodily strength of the malefactor, as well as from the apprehensions of an expected rescue. But the handcuffs which were produced being found too small for the wrists of a man so big-boned as Wilson, Porteous proceeded with his own hands, and by great exertion of strength, to force them till they clasped together, to the exquisite torture of the unhappy criminal. Wilson remonstrated against such barbarous usage, declaring that the pain distracted his thoughts from the subjects of meditation proper to his unhappy condition.

'It signifies little,' replied Captain Porteous, 'Your pain will be soon at an end.'

'Your cruelty is great,' replied the sufferer. 'You know not how soon you yourself may have occasion to ask the mercy, which you are now refusing to a fellow-creature. May God forgive you!'

When the painful procession was completed and Wilson, with the escort, had arrived at the scaffold in the Grassmarket, there appeared no signs of that attempt to rescue him which had occasioned such precautions. There was no attempt at violence. Wilson himself seemed disposed to hasten over the space that divided time from eternity.

The devotions proper and usual on such occasions were no sooner finished than he submitted to his fate, and the sentence of the law was fulfilled.

Sir Walter Scott, 1818

20 God forgive this wretched man! (pairs)

What are the similarities between Fagin's execution and that of Wilson (described in *The Heart of Midlothian*) on page 47?

21 People and places (pairs)

We see Oliver in a variety of locations. Each has a different atmosphere, mood and group of people.

Look back through the extracts from *Oliver Twist,* and chart Oliver's journey. Where, in your opinion, is his natural home?

Fagin in the Condemned Cell

After further adventures, Oliver returns to live with Mr Brownlow. Fagin is caught and condemned to death by hanging. Oliver and Mr Brownlow visit him in prison, but he has lost his mind.

'Fagin,' said the jailer.

'That's me!' cried the Jew, falling, instantly, into the attitude of listening he had assumed upon his trial. 'An old man, my Lord; a very old, old man!'

'Here,' said the turnkey, laying his hand upon his breast to keep him down. 'Here's somebody wants to see you. Fagin, Fagin! Are you a man?'

'I shan't be one long,' he replied, looking up with a face retaining no human expression but rage and terror. 'Strike them all dead! What right have they to butcher me?'

As he spoke he caught sight of Oliver and Mr Brownlow. Shrinking to the farthest corner of the seat, he demanded to know what they wanted there.

'Steady,' said the turnkey, still holding him down. 'Now, sir, tell him what you want. Quick, if you please, for he grows worse as the time gets on.'

'I am not afraid,' said Oliver in a low voice, as he relinquished Mr Brownlow's hand.

'Oliver,' cried Fagin, beckoning to him. 'Here, here! Let me whisper to you. I want to talk to you, my dear. I want to talk to you.'

'Yes, yes,' returned Oliver. 'Let me say a prayer. Do! Let me say one prayer. Say only one, upon your knees, with me, and we will talk till morning.'

'Outside, outside,' replied Fagin, pushing the boy before him towards the door, and looking vacantly over his head. 'Say I've gone to sleep – they'll believe *you*. You can get me out, if you take me so. Now then, now then!'

'Oh! God forgive this wretched man!' cried the boy with a burst of tears.

'That's right, that's right,' said Fagin. 'That'll help us on. This door first. If I shake and tremble, as we pass the gallows, don't you mind, but hurry on. Now, now, now!'

'Have you nothing to ask him, sir?' inquired the turnkey.

'No,' replied Mr Brownlow. 'If I hoped we could recall him to a sense of his position –'

'Nothing will do that, sir,' replied the man, shaking his head. 'You had better leave him.'

The door of the cell opened, and the attendants returned.

The men laid hands upon him, and disengaging Oliver from his grasp, held him back. He struggled with the power of desperation, for an instant; and then sent up cry upon cry that penetrated even those massive walls, and rang in their ears until they reached the open yard.

Day was dawning when they again emerged. A great multitude had already assembled; the windows were filled with people, smoking and playing cards to beguile the time; the crowd were pushing, quarrelling, joking. Everything told of life and animation, but one dark cluster of objects in the centre of all – the black stage, the cross-beam, the rope, and all the hideous apparatus of death.

DAVID COPPERFIELD

Some Amazing Characters

1 Matching pictures and people (pairs)

In *David Copperfield* you'll meet some amazing characters.

- Look at the artist's impressions on the opposite page and match them to the descriptions below.
- You'll notice there are more descriptions than pictures. Draw a caricature (an exaggerated picture) for the remaining one.

Uriah Heep
His name gives you a clue to his personality. Try saying the name in different ways. Does it sound pleasant? Dickens describes him as 'cadaverous' and 'high-shouldered and bony'. He's always listening at doors and creeping about.

Mr Murdstone
He becomes David Copperfield's stepfather. He is tall and stern with black hair, whiskers and 'ill-omened black eyes'.

Betsey Trotwood
She is David's maiden aunt who is upright and prim. She can be bossy and formidable but really has a kind heart.

Mr Micawber
He is optimistic and cheerful, and even though he never has enough money he always says, 'something will turn up'. Dickens tells us there is 'no more hair upon his head ... than there is upon an egg.'

Peggotty
She is kindly, motherly and smiling; she is a servant who is honest and loyal, always there in times of trouble.

2 'It's a boy' (groups of three)

Read pages 53–55. Use the suggestions below to turn your favourite section of the text into a storyboard for a film.

- Focus on three dramatic moments.
- Consider lighting, sound effects and movement of characters.
- Try to use some quotation in the dialogue you create.
- See page 40 for a detailed example of storyboarding.

3 Contrasting characters (two pairs)

In pairs, choose *either* Betsey Trotwood *or* David's mother, Clara and use the spider diagram below to structure a character analysis.

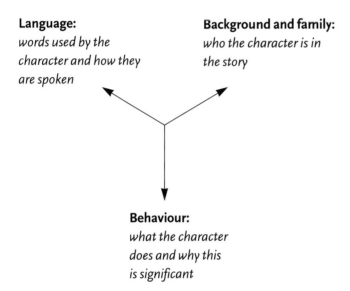

Language:
*words used by the
character and how they
are spoken*

Background and family:
*who the character is in
the story*

Behaviour:
*what the character
does and why this
is significant*

Discuss your pair's findings and work with another pair to answer the following essay question:

- How do Betsey Trotwood's and Clara's characters contrast with each other?

David's Birth

On the night of David Copperfield's birth his widowed mother is visited by her sister-in-law, Betsey Trotwood, who is convinced that the baby will be a girl. The women have not met before.

My mother was sitting by the fire, but poorly in health, and very low in spirits, looking at it through her tears, and desponding heavily about herself and the fatherless little stranger, who was already welcomed by some grosses of prophetic pins, in a drawer upstairs, to a world not at all excited on the subject of his arrival; my mother, I say, was sitting by the fire, that bright, windy March afternoon, very timid and sad, and very doubtful of ever coming alive out of the trial that was before her, when, lifting her eyes as she dried them, to the window opposite, she saw a strange lady coming up the garden.

My mother had a sure foreboding at the second glance, that it was Miss Betsey. The setting sun was glowing on the strange lady, over the garden-fence, and she came walking up to the door with a fell rigidity of figure and composure of countenance that could have belonged to nobody else.

When she reached the house, she gave another proof of her identity. My father had often hinted that she seldom conducted herself like any ordinary Christian; and now, instead of ringing the bell, she came and looked in at that identical window, pressing the end of her nose against the glass to that extent, that my poor dear mother used to say it became perfectly flat and white in a moment.

She gave my mother such a turn, that I have always been convinced I am indebted to Miss Betsey for having been born on a Friday.

They went into the parlour my mother had come from, the fire in the best room on the other side of the passage not being lighted – not having been lighted, indeed, since my father's funeral; and when they were both seated, and Miss Betsey said nothing, my mother, after vainly trying to restrain herself, began to cry.

'Oh tut, tut, tut!' said Miss Betsey, in a hurry. 'Don't do that! Come, come!'

My mother couldn't help it notwithstanding, so she cried until she had had her cry out.

'Take off your cap, child,' said Miss Betsey, 'and let me see you.'

My mother was too much afraid of her to refuse compliance with this odd request, if she had any disposition to do so. Therefore she did as she was told, and did it with such nervous hands that her hair (which was luxuriant and beautiful) fell all about her face.

'Why, bless my heart!' exclaimed Miss Betsey. 'You are a very Baby!'

My mother was, no doubt, unusually youthful in appearance even for her years; she hung her head, as if it were her fault, poor thing, and said, sobbing, that indeed she was afraid she was but a childish widow, and would be but a childish mother if she lived.

'Well?' said Miss Betsey, coming back to her chair, as if she had only been taking a

CONTINUED ☞

David's Birth (continued)

casual look at the prospect; 'and when do you expect – '

'I am all in a tremble,' faltered my mother. 'I don't know what's the matter. I shall die, I am sure!'

'No, no, no,' said Miss Betsey. 'Have some tea.'

'Oh dear me, dear me, do you think it will do me any good?' cried my mother in a helpless manner.

'Of course it will,' said Miss Betsey. 'It's nothing but fancy. What do you call your girl?'

'I don't know that it will be a girl, yet, ma'am,' said my mother innocently.

'Bless the Baby!' exclaimed Miss Betsey, 'I don't mean that. I mean your servant-girl.'

'Peggotty,' said my mother.

'Peggotty!' repeated Miss Betsey, with some indignation. 'Do you mean to say, child, that any human being has gone into a Christian church, and got herself named Peggotty?'

'It's her surname,' said my mother, faintly. 'Mr Copperfield called her by it, because her Christian name was the same as mine.'

'Here! Peggotty!' cried Miss Betsey, opening the parlour-door. 'Tea. Your mistress is a little unwell. Don't dawdle.'

'You were speaking about its being a girl,' said Miss Betsey. 'I have no doubt it will be a girl. I have a presentiment that it must be a girl. Now child, from the moment of the birth of this girl – '

'Perhaps boy,' my mother took the liberty of putting in.

'I tell you I have a presentiment that it must be a girl,' returned Miss Betsey. 'Don't contradict. From the moment of this girl's birth, child, I intend to be her friend. I intend to be her godmother, and I beg you'll call her Betsey Trotwood Copperfield. There must be no mistakes in life with *this* Betsey Trotwood. There must be no trifling with *her* affections, poor dear. She must be well brought up, and well guarded from reposing any foolish confidences where they are not deserved. I must make that *my* care.'

'And was David good to you, child?' asked Miss Betsey, when she had been silent for a little while, and the motions of her head had gradually ceased. 'Were you comfortable together?'

'We were very happy,' said my mother. 'Mr Copperfield was only too good to me.'

'What, he spoilt you, I suppose?' returned Miss Betsey.

'– I kept my housekeeping-book regularly, and balanced it with Mr Copperfield every night,' cried my mother in another burst of distress, and breaking down again.

'Well, well!' said Miss Betsey. 'Don't cry any more.'

'– And I am sure we never had a word of difference respecting it, except when Mr Copperfield objected to my threes and fives being too much like each other, or to my putting curly tails to my sevens and nines,' resumed my mother in another burst, and breaking down again.

David's Birth (continued)

'You'll make yourself ill,' said Miss Betsey, 'and you know that will not be good either for you or for my god-daughter. Come! You mustn't do it!'

My mother was so much worse that Peggotty, coming in with the teaboard and candles, and seeing at a glance how ill she was – as Miss Betsey might have done sooner if there had been light enough – conveyed her upstairs to her own room with all speed; and immediately dispatched Ham Peggotty, her nephew, who had been for some days past secreted in the house, unknown to my mother, as a special messenger in case of emergency, to fetch the nurse and doctor.

'How is she?' said my aunt, folding her arms with her bonnet still tied on one of them.

'Well, ma'am, she will soon be quite comfortable, I hope,' returned Mr Chillip.* 'Quite as comfortable as we can expect a young mother to be, under these melancholy domestic circumstances. There cannot be any objection to your seeing her presently, ma'am. It may do her good.'

'And *she*. How is *she*?' said my aunt, sharply.

Mr Chillip laid his head a little more on one side, and looked at my aunt like an amiable bird.

'The baby,' said my aunt. 'How is she?'

'Ma'am,' returned Mr Chillip, 'I apprehended you had known. It's a boy.'

My aunt said never a word, but took her bonnet by the strings, in the manner of a sling, aimed a blow at Mr Chillip's head with it, put it on bent, walked out, and never came back. She vanished like a discontented fairy; or like one of those supernatural beings, whom it was popularly supposed I was entitled to see; and never came back any more.

* Mr Chillip: the doctor

4 'Do plants eat soil?' (pairs)

What questions do young children ask adults about the world about them? How do adults try to answer them?

Improvise a scene between a child who asks the question 'Do plants eat soil?' and an adult who tries to answer. Then read page 57. What question does David ask and what are his reasons for asking?

5 'By the parlour fire' (pairs)

How does Dickens create a calm atmosphere and give the reader a sense of David's security?

Use the questions on the spider diagram below to structure your evidence.

Action –
What actually happens?
What movements or
changes happen?

Character interaction –
What is the dialogue for?
Is it giving information, instructions or
for discussion? What is the effect of this?

Emotions –
What feelings are expressed
in the passage? How does
the language reflect this?
Why is the ending
humorous?

Style –
Are the sentences doing, describing
or speaking (dialogue)?
Are the sentences short and sharp, or long and
complex (made up of phrases joined together)?
What is the effect of this?

Peggotty

Mrs Copperfield's servant, Peggotty, takes charge of David's welfare and becomes his friend. In many ways she is a substitute mother to David.

Peggotty and I were sitting one night by the parlour fire, alone. I had been reading to Peggotty about crocodiles. I must have read very perspicuously, or the good soul must have been deeply interested, for I remember she had a cloudy impression, after I had done, that they were a sort of vegetable. I was tired of reading, and dead sleepy; but having leave, as a high treat, to sit up until my mother came home from spending the evening at a neighbour's, I would rather have died upon my post (of course) than have gone to bed.

'Peggotty,' says I, suddenly, 'were you ever married?'

'Lord, Master Davy,' replied Peggotty. 'What's put marriage in your head?'

She answered with such a start, that it quite awoke me. And then she stopped in her work, and looked at me, with her needle drawn out to its thread's length.

'But *were* you ever married, Peggotty?' says I. 'You are a very handsome woman, an't you?'

I thought her in a different style from my mother, certainly; but of another school of beauty, I considered her a perfect example. There was a red velvet footstool in the best parlour, on which my mother had painted a nosegay. The ground-work of that stool, and Peggotty's complexion, appeared to me to be one and the same thing. The stool was smooth, and Peggotty was rough, but that made no difference.

'*Me* handsome, Davy!' said Peggotty. 'Lawk, no, my dear! But what put marriage in your head?'

'I don't know – You mustn't marry more than one person at a time, may you, Peggotty?'

'Certainly not,' says Peggotty, with the promptest decision.

'But if you marry a person, and the person dies, why then you may marry another person, mayn't you, Peggotty?'

'You *may*,' says Peggotty, 'if you choose, my dear. That's a matter of opinion.'

'But what is your opinion, Peggotty?' said I.

I asked her, and looked curiously at her, because she looked so curiously at me.

'My opinion is,' said Peggotty, taking her eyes from me, after a little indecision and going on with her work, 'that I never was married myself, Master Davy, and that I don't expect to be. That's all I know about the subject.'

'You an't cross, I suppose, Peggotty, are you?' said I, after sitting quiet for a minute.

I really thought she was, she had been so short with me; but I was quite mistaken: for she laid aside her work (which was a stocking of her own), and opening her arms wide, took my curly head within them, and gave it a good squeeze. I knew it was a good squeeze, because, being very plump, whenever she made any little exertion after she was dressed, some of the buttons on the back of her gown flew off. And I recollect two bursting to the opposite side of the parlour, while she was hugging me.

6 The first visit (groups of five)

One of you invites a friend to meet the family for the first time. Improvise the scene.

Note down the incidents and questions that show this is David's first visit to the boat-house.

7 Aladdin's cave (pairs)

Peggotty's family live in an upturned boat on the beach at Yarmouth. David sees it as a fairytale place. Dickens uses a number of techniques to show David's fascination with the Peggotty household and where they live. Use the spider diagram below to find evidence of these in the passage.

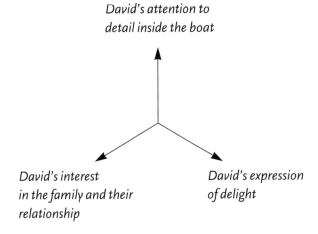

David's attention to detail inside the boat

David's interest in the family and their relationship

David's expression of delight

8 'That ship-looking thing' (individual)

David is 'charmed' by such an unusual home. Imagine you have visited a family living somewhere that has not been designed as a house. Write an account of your visit, using all three of Dickens' techniques to show your fascination with the house and its occupants.

Peggotty's Family at Yarmouth

Peggotty takes David for a fortnight's holiday to stay in Yarmouth with her family, who are an amusing, eccentric group. They live in a strange, delightful 'house'.

'Yon's our house, Mas'r Davy!'

I looked in all directions, as far as I could stare over the wilderness, and away at the sea, and away at the river, but no house could *I* make out. There was a black barge, or some other kind of superannuated boat, not far off, high and dry on the ground, with an iron funnel sticking out of it for a chimney and smoking very cosily; but nothing else in the way of a habitation that was visible to *me*.

'That's not it?' said I. 'That ship-looking thing?'

'That's it, Mas'r Davy,' returned Ham.

If it had been Aladdin's palace, I suppose I could not have been more charmed with the romantic idea of living in it. There was a delightful door cut in the side, and it was roofed in, and there were little windows in it; but the wonderful charm of it was, that it was a real boat which had no doubt been upon the water hundreds of times, and which had never been intended to be lived in, on dry land. That was the captivation of it to me. If it had ever been meant to be lived in, I might have thought it small, or inconvenient, or lonely; but never having been designed for any such use, it became a perfect abode.

It was beautifully clean inside, and as tidy as possible. There was a table, and a Dutch clock, and a chest of drawers, and on the chest of drawers there was a tea-tray with a painting on it of a lady with a parasol, taking a walk with a military-looking child who was trundling a hoop. The tray was kept from tumbling down, by a Bible; and the tray, if it had tumbled down, would have smashed a quantity of cups and saucers and a teapot that were grouped around the book. On the walls there were some common coloured pictures, framed and glazed, of Scripture subjects; such as I have never seen since in the hands of pedlars, without seeing the whole

CONTINUED ☞

Peggotty's Family at Yarmouth (continued)

interior of Peggotty's brother's house again, at one view. Abraham in red going to sacrifice Isaac in blue, and Daniel in yellow cast into a den of green lions, were the most prominent of these.

Over the little mantel-shelf, was a picture of the Sarah Jane lugger, built at Sunderland, with a real little wooden stern stuck on to it; a work of art, combining composition with carpentry, which I considered to be one of the most enviable possessions that the world could afford. There were some hooks in the beams of the ceiling, the use of which I did not divine then; and some lockers and boxes and conveniences of that sort, which served for seats and eked out the chairs.

We were welcomed by a very civil woman in a white apron, whom I had seen curtseying at the door when I was on Ham's back, about a quarter of a mile off. Likewise by a most beautiful little girl (or I thought her so) with a necklace of blue beads on, who wouldn't let me kiss her when I offered to, but ran away and hid herself.

By-and-by, when we had dined in a sumptuous manner off boiled dabs, melted butter, and potatoes, with a chop for me, a hairy man with a very good-natured face came home. As he called Peggotty 'Lass', and gave her a hearty smack on the cheek, I had no doubt, from the general propriety of her conduct, that he was her brother; and so he turned out – being presently introduced to me as Mr Peggotty, the master of the house.

'Glad to see you, sir,' said Mr Peggotty. 'You'll find us rough, sir, but you'll find us ready.'

I thanked him, and replied that I was sure I should be happy in such a delightful place.

'How's your Ma, sir,' said Mr Peggotty. 'Did you leave her pretty jolly?'

I gave Mr Peggotty to understand that she was as jolly as I could wish, and that she desired her compliments – which was a polite fiction on my part.

'I'm much obleeged to her, I'm sure,' said Mr Peggotty. 'Well, sir, if you can make out here, fur a fortnut, 'long wi' her,' nodding at his sister, 'and Ham, and little Em'ly, we shall be proud of your company.'

Having done the honours of his house in this hospitable manner, Mr Peggotty went out to wash himself in a kettleful of hot water, remarking that 'cold would never get *his* muck off.' He soon returned, greatly improved in appearance; but so rubicund, that I couldn't help thinking his face had this in common with the lobsters, crabs, and crawfish* – that it went into the hot water very black, and came out very red.

After tea, when the door was shut and all was made snug (the nights being cold and misty now), it seemed to me the most delicious retreat that the imagination of man could conceive. To hear the wind getting up out at sea, to know that the fog was creeping over the desolate flat outside, and to look at the fire, and think that there was no house near but this one, and this one a boat, was like enchantment. Little Em'ly had overcome her shyness, and was sitting by my side upon the lowest and least of the lockers, which was just large enough for us two, and just fitted into the chimney-corner. Mrs Peggotty with the white apron, was knitting on the opposite side of the fire.

Mr Peggotty was smoking his pipe. I felt it was a time for conversation and confidence.

'Mr Peggotty!' says I.

'Sir,' says he.

* crayfish

Peggotty's Family at Yarmouth (continued)

'Did you give your son the name of Ham, because you lived in a sort of ark?'

Mr Peggotty seemed to think it a deep idea, but answered:

'No, sir. I never giv him no name.'

'Who gave him that name, then?' said I, putting question number two of the catechism to Mr Peggotty.

'Why, sir, his father giv it to him,' said Mr Peggotty.

'I thought you were his father!'

'My brother Joe was *his* father,' said Mr Peggotty.

'Dead, Mr Peggotty?' I hinted, after a respectful pause.

'Drowndead,' said Mr Peggotty.

I was very much surprised that Mr Peggotty was not Ham's father, and began to wonder whether I was mistaken about his relationship to anybody else there. I was so curious to know, that I made up my mind to have it out with Mr Peggotty.

'Little Em'ly,' I said, glancing at her. 'She is your daughter, isn't she, Mr Peggotty?'

'No, sir. My brother-in-law, Tom, was *her* father.'

I couldn't help it. '– Dead, Mr Peggotty?' I hinted, after another respectful silence.

'Drowndead,' said Mr Peggotty.

I felt the difficulty of resuming the subject, but had not got to the bottom of it yet, and must get to the bottom somehow. So I said:

'Haven't you *any* children, Mr Peggotty?'

'No, master,' he answered with a short laugh. 'I'm a bacheldore.'

'A bachelor!' I said, astonished. 'Why, who's that, Mr Peggotty?' Pointing to the person in the apron who was knitting.

'That's Missis Gummidge,' said Mr Peggotty.

'Gummidge, Mr Peggotty?'

But at this point Peggotty – I mean my own peculiar Peggotty – made such impressive motions to me not to ask any more questions, that I could only sit and look at all the silent company, until it was time to go to bed. Then, in the privacy of my own little cabin, she informed me that Ham and Em'ly were an orphan nephew and niece, whom my host had at different times adopted in their childhood, when they were left destitute; and that Mrs Gummidge was the widow of his partner in a boat, who had died very poor. He was but a poor man himself, said Peggotty, but as good as gold and as true as steel – those were her similes.

I was very sensible of my host's goodness, and listened to the women's going to bed in another little crib like mine at the opposite end of the boat, and to him and Ham hanging up two hammocks for themselves on the hooks I had noticed in the roof, in a very luxurious state of mind, enhanced by my being sleepy. As slumber gradually stole upon me, I heard the wind howling out at sea and coming on across the flat so fiercely, that I had a lazy apprehension of the great deep rising in the night. But I bethought myself that I was in a boat, after all; and that a man like Mr Peggotty was not a bad person to have on board if anything did happen.

9 Dickens' sentence structure and its effect (individual)

This passage charts a turning point in David's life. Mr Murdstone's harsh approach shocks David into a violent reaction. The sentence structure shows the build-up of tension and emotion. Look carefully at the difference between the calm, descriptive sentences at the beginning and the disjointed, broken sentences later in the passage.

Use a copy of this column plan to gather evidence.

Types of sentence	Example	Effect
Descriptive	'One morning …'	Build-up of detail Scene-setting
Short dialogue		
Exclamatory sentences	'Don't! Pray don't beat me!'	
Disjointed sentences		Increase of nervous tension

10 Discipline (two pairs)

Mr Murdstone and David's mother disagree on how to bring up children.

Each pair represents the views of *either* Mr Murdstone *or* David's mother. Imagine you have been asked to explain to a social worker your approach to discipline. Prepare your case, considering the following points:

- How do you feel David has been behaving?
- What should be done?
- Why do you hold these opinions?

David Bites Mr Murdstone

When David returns from Yarmouth he finds that his mother has remarried. Her new husband Mr Murdstone has moved in with his strict sister who takes over the housekeeping. David finds his stepfather harsh and unpleasant.

One morning when I went into the parlour with my books, I found my mother looking anxious, Miss Murdstone looking firm, and Mr Murdstone with a lithe and limber cane, which he poised and switched in the air.

'I tell you, Clara,' said Mr Murdstone, 'I have been often flogged myself.'

'To be sure; of course,' said Miss Murdstone.

'Certainly, my dear Jane,' faltered my mother, meekly. 'But – but do you think it did Edward good?'

'Do you think it did me harm, Clara?' asked Mr Murdstone, gravely.

I felt an apprehension that I was personally interested in this dialogue, and sought Mr Murdstone's eye as it lighted on mine.

'Now, David,' he said, 'you must be far more careful today than usual.' He gave the cane another poise, and another switch; and having finished his preparation of it, laid it down beside him, with an expressive look, and took up a book.

This was a good freshener to my presence of mind, as a beginning. I felt the words of my lessons slipping off, not one by one, or line by line, but by the entire page. I tried to lay hold of them; but they seemed, if I may so express it, to have put skates on, and to skim away from me with a smoothness there was no checking.

We began badly, and went on worse. I had come in, conceiving that I was very well prepared; but it turned out to be quite a mistake. Book after book was added to the heap of failures. My mother burst out crying.

'Clara!' said Miss Murdstone, in her warning voice.

'I am not quite well, my dear Jane, I think,' said my mother.

I saw him wink, solemnly, at his sister, as he rose and said, taking up the cane: 'David, you and I will go upstairs, boy.'

He walked me up to my room slowly and gravely, and when we got there, suddenly twisted my head under his arm.

'Mr Murdstone! Sir!' I cried to him. 'Don't! Pray don't beat me! I have tried to learn, sir, but I can't learn when you and Miss Murdstone are by. I can't indeed!'

'Can't you, indeed, David?' he said. 'We'll try that.'

He had my head as in a vice, but I twined round him somehow, and stopped him for a moment, entreating him not to beat me. It was only for a moment that I stopped him, for he cut me heavily an instant afterwards, and in the same instant I caught the hand with which he held me in my mouth, between my teeth, and bit it through.

He beat me then, as if he would have beaten me to death. Above all the noise we made, I heard them running up the stairs, and crying out – I heard my mother crying out – and Peggotty. Then he was gone; and the door was locked outside; and I was lying, fevered and hot, and torn, and sore, and raging in my puny way, upon the floor.

11 An unjust punishment (pairs)

Several Victorian novelists show childhood characters being unjustly punished. Jane Eyre is a young orphan who is being bullied by her cousin John. In this extract Charlotte Brontë varies her sentence structure in a similar way to Dickens in his description of David biting Mr Murdstone (page 63).

First read the passage from *Jane Eyre* aloud. Then:

- Draw and complete a column plan similar to the one on page 38.
- Use the plan to write an essay:
  'How Dickens and Brontë use similar techniques to create atmosphere in *David Copperfield* and *Jane Eyre*.'

12 Learning (individual)

How do the two characters feel about education?

David Copperfield's attitude to education	Jane Eyre's attitude to education
Forced to learn. Fear of failure …	Loves reading; reads complicated books. Makes connections between things she has read, and real-life situations. Uses learning as a weapon.

Jane Eyre

'What were you doing behind the curtain?' John asked.

'I was reading.'

'Show the book.'

I returned to the window and fetched it thence.

'You have no business to take our books; you are a dependant, mamma says. You have no money ; your father left you none; you ought to beg, and not to live here with gentlemen's children like us, and eat the same meals we do, and wear clothes at our mamma's expense. Now, I'll teach you to rummage my book-shelves: for they *are* mine; all the house belongs to me, or will do in a few years. Go and stand by the door, out of the way of the mirror and the windows.'

I did so, not at first aware what was his intention; but when I saw him lift and poise the book and stand in act to hurl it, I instinctively started aside with a cry of alarm: not soon enough, however; the volume was flung, it hit me, and I fell, striking my head against the door and cutting it. The cut bled, the pain was sharp: my terror had passed its climax; other feelings succeeded.

'Wicked and cruel boy!' I said. 'You are like a murderer – you are like a slave-driver – you are like the Roman emperors!'

I had read Goldsmith's *History of Rome*, and had formed my opinion of Nero, Caligula, etc. Also I had drawn parallels in silence, which I never thought thus to have declared aloud.

'What! what!' he cried. 'Did she say that to me? Did you hear her, Eliza and Georgiana? Won't I tell mamma? but first –'

He ran headlong at me: I felt him grasp my hair and my shoulder: he had closed with a desperate thing. I really saw in him a tyrant: a murderer. I felt a drop or two of blood from my head trickle down my neck, and was sensible of somewhat pungent suffering: these sensations for the time predominated over fear, and I received him in frantic sort. I don't very well know what I did with my hands, but he called me 'Rat! rat!' and bellowed out aloud. Aid was near him: Eliza and Georgiana had run for Mrs Reed, who was gone upstairs; she now came upon the scene, followed by Bessie and her maid Abbot. We were parted: I heard the words –

'Dear! dear! What a fury to fly at Master John!'

'Did ever anybody see such a picture of passion!'

Then Mrs Reed subjoined: 'Take her away to the red-room, and lock her in there.' Four hands were immediately laid upon me, and I was borne upstairs.

Charlotte Brontë, 1847

13 Advice (groups of three)

David is renting a room in Mr Micawber's house. He is given two pieces of advice by Mr Micawber.

- Take parts as narrator, Mr and Mrs Micawber, and read page 67 aloud.
- Choose one piece of advice given by Mr Micawber and create a scene where someone is given the advice but ignores it.

14 'The miserable wretch you behold' (pairs)

Mr Micawber gives advice with a 'flourish'. One definition of *flourish* is 'a florid verbal embellishment'. This suggests that his language is designed to impress and is deliberately constructed in stages. The chart below analyses how Mr Micawber gives his messages. Copy and complete it.

Advice	'Never do tomorrow what you can do today.'	' My other piece of advice ...'
Next comment	Turns it into a maxim (a short, generalised saying): 'Procras ...'	
Following messages	Discusses marriage, as an example.	

Mr Micawber Gives David some Advice

After biting Mr Murdstone, David is sent to boarding school for a while, and then to work in Mr Murdstone's warehouse in London. While there he meets Mr Micawber, an optimistic, generous character who is often in debt and prone to deep but short-lived depression.

'My dear young friend,' said Mr Micawber, 'I am older than you; a man of some experience in life, and – and of some experience, in short, in difficulties, generally speaking. At present, and until something turns up (which I am, I may say, hourly expecting), I have nothing to bestow but advice. Still my advice is so far worth taking, that – in short, that I have never taken it myself, and am the' – here Mr Micawber, who had been beaming and smiling, all over his head and face, up to the present moment, checked himself and frowned – 'the miserable wretch you behold.'

'My dear Micawber!' urged his wife.

'I say,' returned Mr Micawber, quite forgetting himself, and smiling again, 'the miserable wretch you behold. My advice is, never do tomorrow what you can do today. Procrastination is the thief of time. Collar him!'

'My poor papa's maxim,' Mrs Micawber observed.

'My dear,' said Mr Micawber, 'your papa was very well in his way, and Heaven forbid that I should disparage him. Take him for all in all, we ne'er shall – in short, make the acquaintance, probably, of anybody else possessing, at his time of life, the same legs for gaiters, and able to read the same description of print, without spectacles. But he applied that maxim to our marriage, my dear; and that was so far prematurely entered into, in consequence, that I never recovered the expense.'

Mr Micawber looked aside at Mrs Micawber, and added: 'Not that I am sorry for it. Quite the contrary, my love.' After which, he was grave for a minute or so.

'My other piece of advice, Copperfield,' said Mr Micawber, 'you know. Annual income twenty pounds, annual expenditure nineteen nineteen six, result happiness. Annual income twenty pounds, annual expenditure twenty pounds ought and six, result misery. The blossom is blighted, the leaf is withered, the God of day goes down upon the dreary scene, and – and in short you are forever floored. As I am!'

To make his example the more impressive, Mr Micawber drank a glass of punch with an air of great enjoyment and satisfaction, and whistled the College Hornpipe.

15 What I say and what I do (groups of three)

Sometimes people don't tell the truth about their abilities, ambitions or interests.

- Improvise a scene where someone's dishonesty becomes clear.
- Discuss the reasons for the dishonesty.
- As you read page 69 what signs are there that Uriah Heep is dishonest?

16 The eye of the camera (groups of four)

Uriah Heep works in the same office as David Copperfield. Dickens' description of him uses a combination of cinematic, visual and sensory (appealing to the senses) techniques to show his character. Use a chart like this to define his character.

Techniques	Examples	What is shown about his character
Cinematic	*Focuses on details like Uriah's mouth …*	*Attention to detail.*
Sensory	*Uriah traces the words in the text, reading with a 'lank forefinger, like a snail'. He frequently wipes his damp hands.*	*This makes Uriah seem nervous, as if he is …*

17 Uriah's speech (pairs)

Uriah drops the letter 'h' when he speaks. What does this show about him?

Uriah Heep

David finds a job at a lawyer's office in Canterbury where he meets the hypocritical clerk Uriah Heep.

'You are working late tonight, Uriah,' says I.

'Yes, Master Copperfield,' says Uriah.

As I was getting on the stool opposite, to talk to him more conveniently, I observed that he had not such a thing as a smile about him, and that he could only widen his mouth and make two hard creases down his cheeks, one on each side, to stand for one.

'I am not doing office-work, Master Copperfield,' said Uriah.

'What work, then?' I asked.

'I am improving my legal knowledge, Master Copperfield,' said Uriah. 'I am going through 'Tidd's Practice'.* Oh, what a writer Mr Tidd is, Master Copperfield!'

My stool was such a tower of observation, that as I watched him reading on again, after this rapturous exclamation, and following up the lines with his forefinger, I observed that his nostrils, which were thin and pinched, with sharp dints in them, had a singular and most uncomfortable way of expanding and contracting themselves – that they seemed to twinkle, instead of his eyes, which hardly ever twinkled at all.

'I suppose you are quite a great lawyer?' I said, after looking at him for some time.

'Me, Master Copperfield?' said Uriah. 'Oh, no! I'm a very umble person.'

It was no fancy of mine about his hands, I observed; for he frequently ground the palms against each other as if to squeeze them dry and warm, besides often wiping them, in a stealthy way, on his pocket-handkerchief.

'I am well aware that I am the umblest person going,' said Uriah Heep, modestly; 'let the other be where he may. My mother is likewise a very umble person. We live in a numble abode, Master Copperfield, but have much to be thankful for. My father's former calling was umble. He was a sexton.'

'What is he now?' I asked.

'He is a partaker of glory at present, Master Copperfield,' said Uriah Heep. 'But we have much to be thankful for. How much have I to be thankful for, in living with Mr Wickfield!'

I asked Uriah if he had been with Mr Wickfield long.

'I have been with him, going on four year, Master Copperfield,' said Uriah; shutting up his book, after carefully marking the place where he had left off. 'Since a year after my father's death. How much have I to be thankful for, in that! How much have I to be thankful for, in Mr Wickfield's kind intention to give me my articles which would otherwise not lay within the umble means of mother and self!'

'Then, when your articled time is over, you'll be a regular lawyer, I suppose?' said I.

'With the blessing of Providence, Master Copperfield,' returned Uriah.

* 'Tidd's Practice' was a legal handbook.

18 Some amazing characters (groups of four)

Dickens brings some amazing characters to life in *David Copperfield*.
David's aunt Betsey Trotwood (page 53) was present as he was born at the
opening of the story. She returns to the story when David runs away from
Mr Murdstone's beatings.

Read pages 71–73. Then choose one of the scenes below and create a short
drama which shows the individuality of the characters through what they
say and what they do.

- David's arrival at his aunt's home.
- Betsey Trotwood's war against the donkeys.
- Mr Dick and David.

19 Where should David live? (groups of seven)

- Peggotty
- David
- Mr Murdstone
- David's mother
- Mr Micawber
- Uriah Heep
- The social worker

Imagine that a social worker has called a family conference to decide where
David should live. Choose a character each from the list above and prepare
notes on why you are the best person to take care of David. The social
worker should prepare questions to ask each character.

Issues to consider include:

- Events that have happened.
- People's characters and relationships.
- What is in David's best interests.

Some Amazing Characters

*After David's mother dies, he decides to find his only living relative, the aunt, Betsey
Trotwood who was in the house when he was born. He walks from London to Dover,
spending nights in the open and selling his clothes to buy food.*

'If you please, aunt.'

'Eh?' exclaimed Miss Betsey, in a tone of amazement I have never heard
approached.

'If you please, aunt, I am your nephew.'

'Oh, Lord!' said my aunt. And sat flat down in the garden-path.

'I am David Copperfield, of Blunderstone, in Suffolk – where you came, on the
night when I was born, and saw my dear mama. I have been very unhappy since she
died. I have been slighted, and taught nothing, and thrown upon myself, and put to
work not fit for me. It made me run away to you. I was robbed at first setting out, and
have walked all the way, and have never slept in a bed since I began the journey.' Here
my self-support gave way all at once; and with a movement of my hands, intended to
show her my ragged state, and call it to witness that I had suffered something, I
broke into a passion of crying, which I suppose had been pent up within me all the
week.

My aunt sat on the gravel, staring at me, until I began to cry; when she got up in a
great hurry, collared me, and took me into the parlour. Her first proceeding there was
to unlock a tall press, bring out several bottles, and pour some of the contents of
each into my mouth. I think they must have been taken out at random, for I am sure
I tasted aniseed water, anchovy sauce, and salad dressing. When she had
administered these restoratives, as I was still quite hysterical, and unable to control
my sobs, she put me on the sofa, with a shawl under my head, and the handkerchief
from her own head under my feet, lest I should sully the cover; and then, sitting
herself down behind a green fan or screen, so that I could not see her face, exclaimed
at intervals 'Mercy on us!' letting those exclamations off like minute guns.

After a time she rang the bell. 'Janet,' said my aunt, when her servant came in. 'Go
upstairs, give my compliments to Mr Dick, and say I wish to speak to him.'

Janet looked a little surprised to see me lying stiffly on the sofa (I was afraid to
move lest it should be displeasing to my aunt), but went on her errand. My aunt, with
her hands behind her, walked up and down the room, until the gentleman who had
squinted at me from the upper window came in laughing.

'Mr Dick,' said my aunt, 'don't be a fool, because nobody can be more discreet
than you can, when you choose. We all know that. So don't be a fool, whatever you
are.'

The gentleman was serious immediately, and looked at me, I thought, as if he
would entreat me to say nothing about the window.

'Mr Dick,' said my aunt, 'you have heard me mention David Copperfield? Now
don't pretend not to have a memory, because you and I know better.'

CONTINUED ☞

Some Amazing Characters (continued)

'David Copperfield?' said Mr Dick, who did not appear to me to remember much about it. '*David* Copperfield? Oh yes, to be sure. David, certainly.'

'Well,' said my aunt, 'this is his boy – his son. He would be as like his father as it's possible to be, if he was not so like his mother, too.'

'His son?' said Mr Dick. 'David's son? Indeed!'

'Yes,' pursued my aunt, 'and he has done a pretty piece of business. He has run away. How can you pretend to be wool-gathering, Dick, when you are as sharp as a surgeon's lancet? Now, here you see young David Copperfield, and the question I put to you is, what shall I do with him?'

'What shall you do with him?' said Mr Dick, feebly, scratching his head. 'Oh! do with him?'

'Yes,' said my aunt, with a grave look and her forefinger held up. 'Come! I want some sound advice.'

'Why, if I was you,' said Mr Dick, considering, and looking vacantly at me, 'I should –' The contemplation of me seemed to inspire him with a sudden idea, and he added, briskly, 'I should wash him!'

'Janet,' said my aunt, turning round with a quiet triumph, which I did not then understand, 'Mr Dick sets us all right. Heat the bath!'

Janet had gone away to get the bath ready, when my aunt, to my great alarm, became in one moment rigid with indignation, and had hardly voice to cry out, 'Janet! Donkeys!'

Upon which, Janet came running up the stairs as if the house were in flames, darted out on a little piece of green in front, and warned off two saddle-donkeys, lady-ridden, that had presumed to set hoof upon it; while my aunt, rushing out of the house, seized the bridle of a third animal laden with a bestriding child, turned him, led him forth from those sacred precincts, and boxed the ears of the unlucky urchin in attendance who had dared to profane that hallowed ground.

To this hour I don't know whether my aunt had any lawful right of way over that patch of green; but she had settled it in her own mind that she had, and it was all the same to her. The one great outrage of her life, demanding to be constantly avenged, was the passage of a donkey over that immaculate spot. In whatever occupation she was engaged, however interesting to her the conversation in which she was taking part, a donkey turned the current of her ideas in a moment, and she was upon him straight. Jugs of water, and watering pots, were kept in secret places ready to be discharged on the offending boys; sticks were laid in ambush behind the door; sallies were made at all hours; and incessant war prevailed.

Mr Dick was grey-headed, and florid: I should have said all about him, in saying so, had not his head been curiously bowed – not by age; it reminded me of one of Mr Creakle's boys' heads after a beating – and his grey eyes prominent and large, with a strange kind of watery brightness in them that made me, in combination with his vacant manner, his submission to my aunt, and his childish delight when she

Some Amazing Characters (continued)

praised him, suspect him of being a little mad; though, if he were mad, how he came to be there puzzled me extremely. He was dressed like any other ordinary gentleman, in a loose grey morning coat and waistcoat, and white trousers; and had his watch in his fob, and his money in his pockets; which he rattled as if he were very proud of it.

'You have been to school?'

'Yes, sir,' I answered; 'for a short time.'

'Do you recollect the date,' said Mr Dick, looking earnestly at me, and taking up his pen to note it down, 'when King Charles the First had his head cut off?'

I said I believed it happened in the year sixteen hundred and forty-nine.

'Well,' returned Mr Dick, scratching his ear with his pen, and looking dubiously at me. 'So the books say; but I don't see how that can be. Because, if it was so long ago, how could the people about him have made that mistake of putting some of the trouble out of *his* head, after it was taken off, into *mine*?'

I was very much surprised by the enquiry; but could give no information on this point.

'It's very strange,' said Mr Dick, with a despondent look upon his papers, and with his hand among his hair again, 'that I never can get that quite right. I never can make that perfectly clear. But no matter, no matter!' he said cheerfully, and rousing himself, 'there's time enough! My compliments to Miss Trotwood, I am getting on very well indeed.'

I was going away, when he directed my attention to the kite.

'What do you think of that for a kite?' he said.

I answered that it was a beautiful one. I should think it must have been as much as seven feet high.

'I made it. We'll go and fly it, you and I,' said Mr Dick. 'Do you see this?'

He showed me that it was covered with manuscript, very closely and laboriously written; but so plainly, that as I looked along the lines, I thought I saw some allusion to King Charles the First's head again, in one or two places.

'There's plenty of string,' said Mr Dick, 'and when it flies high, it takes the facts a long way. That's my manner of diffusing 'em. I don't know where they may come down. It's according to circumstances, and the wind, and so forth; but I take my chance of that.'

His face was so very mild and pleasant, and had something so reverend in it, though it was hale and hearty, that I was not sure but that he was having a good-natured jest with me. So I laughed, and he laughed, and we parted the best friends possible.

GREAT EXPECTATIONS

A Tale with a Twist

The Churchyard

At the start of Great Expectations, Pip, the narrator of the story, is a small child, wandering alone in the churchyard where his parents and five little brothers lie buried, when he has a sudden terrifying encounter with an escaped convict.

My father's family name being Pirrip, and my Christian name Philip, my infant tongue could make of both names nothing longer or more explicit than Pip. So, I called myself Pip, and came to be called Pip.

I give Pirrip as my father's family name, on the authority of his tombstone and my sister Mrs Joe Gargery, who married the blacksmith. As I never saw my father or my mother, and never saw any likeness of either of them (for their days were long before the days of photographs), my first fancies regarding what they were like, were unreasonably derived from their tombstones. The shape of the letters on my father's gave me an odd idea that he was a square, stout, dark man, with curly black hair. From the character and turn of the inscription, 'Also Georgiana Wife of the Above', I drew a childish conclusion that my mother was freckled and sickly. To five little stone lozenges, each about a foot and a half long, which were arranged in a neat row beside their grave, and were sacred to the memory of five little brothers of mine – who gave up trying to get a living exceedingly early in that universal struggle – I am indebted for a belief I religiously entertained that they had all been born on their backs with their hands in their trousers-pockets, and had never taken them out in this state of existence.

Ours was the marsh country, down by the river, within, as the river wound, twenty miles of the sea. My first most vivid and broad impression of the identity of things, seems to me to have been gained on a memorable raw afternoon towards evening. At such a time I found out for certain, that this bleak place overgrown with nettles was the churchyard; and that Philip Pirrip, late of this parish, and also Georgiana wife of the above, were dead and buried; and that Alexander, Bartholomew, Abraham, Tobias and Roger, infant children of the aforesaid, were also dead and buried; and that the dark flat wilderness beyond the churchyard, intersected with dykes and mounds and gates, with scattered cattle feeding on it, was the marshes; and that the low leaden line beyond was the river; and that the distant savage lair from which the wind was rushing, was the sea; and that the small bundle of shivers growing afraid of it all and beginning to cry, was Pip.

'Hold your noise!' cried a terrible voice, as a man started up from among the graves at the side of the church porch. 'Keep still, you little devil, or I'll cut your throat!'

A fearful man, all in coarse gray, with a great iron on his leg. A man with no hat, and with broken shoes, and with an old rag tied round his head. A man who had been soaked in water, and smothered in mud, and lamed by stones, and cut by flints, and stung by nettles, and torn by briars; who limped, and shivered, and glared and growled; and whose teeth chattered in his head as he seized me by the chin.

CONTINUED ☞

The Churchyard (continued)

'Oh! Don't cut my throat, sir,' I pleaded in terror. 'Pray don't do it, sir.'

'Tell us your name!' said the man. 'Quick!'

'Pip, sir.'

'Once more,' said the man, staring at me. 'Give it mouth!'

'Pip. Pip, sir.'

'Show us where you live,' said the man. 'Pint out the place!'

I pointed to where our village lay, on the flat inshore among the alder-trees and pollards, a mile or more from the church.

The man, after looking at me for a moment, turned me upside-down, and emptied my pockets. There was nothing in them but a piece of bread. When the church came to itself – for he was so sudden and strong that he made it go head over heels before me, and I saw the steeple under my feet – when the church came to itself, I say, I was seated on a high tombstone, trembling, while he ate the bread ravenously.

'You young dog,' said the man, licking his lips, 'what fat cheeks you ha'got.'

I believe they were fat, though I was at that time undersized for my years, and not strong.

'Darn me if I couldn't eat 'em,' said the man, with a threatening shake of his head, 'and if I han't half a mind to 't!'

I earnestly expressed my hope that he wouldn't, and held tighter to the tombstone on which he had put me; partly to keep myself upon it; partly, to keep myself from crying.

'Now then, lookee here!' said the man. 'Where's your mother?'

'There, sir!' said I.

He started, made a short run, and stopped and looked over his shoulder.

'There, sir!' I timidly explained. ' "Also Georgiana." That's my mother.'

'Oh!' said he, coming back. 'And is that your father alonger your mother?'

'Yes, sir,' said I; 'him too; late of this parish.'

'Ha!' he muttered then, considering. 'Who d'ye live with supposin' you're kindly let to live, which I han't made up my mind about?'

'My sister, sir. Mrs Joe Gargery, wife of Joe Gargery, the blacksmith, sir.'

'Blacksmith, eh?' said he. And he looked down at his leg.

After darkly looking at his leg and at me several times, he came closer to my tombstone, took me by both arms, tilted me back as far as he could hold me; so that his eyes looked most powerfully down into mine, and mine looked most helplessly up into his.

'Now lookee here,' he said, 'the question being whether you're to be let to live. You know what a file is?'

'Yes, sir.'

'And you know what wittles is?'

'Yes, sir.'

The Churchyard (continued)

After each question he tilted me over a little more, so as to give me a greater sense of helplessness and danger.

'You get me a file.' He tilted me again. 'And you get me wittles.' He tilted me again. 'You bring 'em both to me.' He tilted me again. 'Or I'll have your heart and liver out.' He tilted me again.

I was dreadfully frightened, and so giddy that I clung to him with both hands, and said, 'If you would kindly please to let me keep upright, sir, perhaps I shouldn't be sick, and perhaps I could attend more.'

He gave me a most tremendous dip and roll, so that the church jumped over its own weather-cock. Then, he held me by the arms, in an upright position on the top of the stone, and went on in these fearful terms:

'You bring me, tomorrow morning early, that file and them wittles. You bring the lot to me, at that old Battery over yonder. You do it, and you never dare to say a word or dare to make a sign sumever, and you shall be let to live. You fail, or you go from my words in any partickler, no matter how small it is, and your heart and your liver shall be tore out, roasted and ate. Now, I ain't alone, as you may think I am. There's a young man hid with me, in comparison with which young man I am a Angel. That young man hears the words I speak. That young man has a secret way pecooliar to himself, of getting at a boy, and at his heart, and at his liver. It is in wain for a boy to attempt to hide himself from that young man. A boy may lock his door, may be warm in bed, may tuck himself up, may draw the clothes over his head, may think himself comfortable and safe, but that young man will softly creep and creep his way to him and tear him open. I am a-keeping that young man from harming of you at the present moment, with great difficulty. I find it wery hard to hold that young man off your inside. Now, what do you say?'

I said that I would get him the file, and I would get him what broken bits of food I could, and I would come to him at the Battery, early in the morning.

'Say, Lord strike you dead if you don't!' said the man.

I said so, and he took me down.

'Now,' he pursued, 'you remember what you've undertook, and you remember that young man, and you get home!'

'Goo-good-night, sir,' I faltered.

'Much of that!' said he, glancing about him over the cold wet flat. 'I wish I was a frog. Or a eel!'

At the same time, he hugged his shuddering body in both his arms – clasping himself as if to hold himself together – and limped towards the low church wall. As I saw him go, picking his way among the nettles, and among the brambles that bound the green mounds, he looked in my young eyes as if he were eluding the hands of the dead people, stretching up cautiously out of their graves, to get a twist upon his ankle and pull him in.

CONTINUED ☞

1 A lonely terror (pairs)

One of you is alone in a park feeding the ducks. Suddenly a woman approaches from behind and threatens to push you into the water. What do you do? It's too isolated to shout. You can't swim.

Act out the scene. At the end of your drama, freeze in a tableau to show your fear.

2 Angels and devils (groups of three)

Pip thinks back to his meeting with the convict. One of you is Pip. One is the optimistic 'angel' side of Pip's mind, trying to reassure Pip that all is well. The other is the 'devil' side of Pip's nature, warning of danger.

Copy and complete the chart to help you prepare for the dialogue between the two 'characters'.

Angel	Devil
'Run far and fast! He'll never catch you. He limps, and ...'	'Oh yes he will catch you! Next time you're alone, ...'

3 Creating a mood (pairs)

Writers often make readers understand the feelings of the hero or heroine by reflecting their characters in the description they give of the landscape. This is called *pathetic fallacy*.

How are Pip's feelings reflected in the landscape?

Complete a chart like the one below to help you structure your thoughts about how Dickens uses pathetic fallacy.

How Pip feels	How the scenery shows this
cold and unprotected	'a raw afternoon'
alone	
depressed	'this bleak place'

Decide on a particular mood, for example anger, loneliness or sadness. Then plan and draft a story using pathetic fallacy.

The Churchyard (continued)

When he came to the low church wall, he got over it like a man whose legs were numbed and stiff, and then turned round to look for me. When I saw him turning, I set my face towards home, and made the best use of my legs. But presently I looked over my shoulder, and saw him going on again towards the river, still hugging himself in both arms, and picking his way with his sore feet among the great stones dropped into the marshes here and there, for stepping-places when the rains were heavy, or the tide was in.

The marshes were just a long, black, horizontal line then, as I stopped to look after him; and the river was just another horizontal line, not nearly so broad nor yet so black; and the sky was just a row of long, angry, red lines and dense black lines intermixed. On the edge of the river I could faintly make out the only two black things in all the prospect that seemed to be standing upright; one of these was the beacon by which the sailors steered – like an unhooped cask upon a pole – an ugly thing when you were near it; the other, a gibbet, with some chains hanging to it, which had once held a pirate. The man was limping on towards this latter, as if he were the pirate come to life, and come down, and going back to hook himself up again. It gave me a terrible turn when I thought so; and as I saw the cattle lifting their heads to gaze after him, I wondered whether they thought so too. I looked all round for the horrible young man, and could see no signs of him. But now I was frightened again, and ran home without stopping.

Linked Text

4 Mysteries (pairs)

Great Expectations is a mystery novel. Nothing is what it seems. The convict isn't what he appears, and Pip's life keeps changing. Discuss some of the mysteries at the beginning of the book, then note down your predictions about these points:

- What will become of the lonely orphan Pip?
- Who is the terrifying convict and what does he want?
- In 1860 Dickens wrote that he had 'such a very fine, new and grotesque idea' in *Great Expectations*. What do you suppose that was?

5 'That universal struggle' (groups of three)

Pip describes his brothers' gravestones as 'five little stone lozenges, each about a foot and a half long, ... sacred to the memory of five little brothers of mine'. At the time when Dickens was writing, families often had many children, but many of them died when they were babies. This was because of poor living conditions, especially in towns where the water was polluted and rats ran in the street. Many people had no work and nowhere to live. In winter, people were often found frozen to death. It was not surprising that Pip and his sister were the only survivors of a large family.

- Read 'We are Seven' aloud. One of you read the narrative, the other two speak the dialogue between the little cottage girl and the words of the poet.
- List the similarities between Pip and the little girl in the poem.

6 What should Pip know of death? (pairs)

If Wordsworth had met Pip instead of the little girl, what poem might have been written?

Work together to draft this poem. Keep to the same verse and rhyme scheme as Wordsworth. You might begin:
'I met a little orphan boy ...'

We are seven

A simple child,
That lightly draws its breath,
And feels its life in every limb,
What should it know of death?

I met a little cottage girl;
She was eight years old, she said;
Her hair was thick with many a curl
That clustered round her head.

She had a rustic, woodland air,
And she was wildly clad;
Her eyes were fair, and very fair;
Her beauty made me glad.

'Sisters and brothers, little maid,
How many may you be?'
'How many? Seven in all,' she said,
And wondering looked at me.

'And where are they? I pray you tell.'
She answered, 'Seven are we;
And two of us at Conway dwell,
And two are gone to sea.

'Two of us in the churchyard lie,
My sister and my brother;
And in the churchyard cottage, I,
Dwell near them with my mother.'

'You say that two at Conway dwell,
And two are gone to sea,
Yet ye are seven – I pray you tell,
Sweet maid, how this may be.'

Then did the little maid reply,
'Seven boys and girls are we;
Two of us in the churchyard lie,
Beneath the churchyard tree.'

'You run about, my little maid,
Your limbs they are alive;
If two are in the churchyard laid
Then ye are only five.'

'Their graves are green, they may be seen,'
The little maid replied,
'Twelve steps or more from my mother's door,
And they are side by side.

'My stockings there I often knit,
My kerchief there I hem,
And there upon the ground I sit –
I sit and sing to them.'

'And often after sunset, sir,
When it is light and fair,
I take my little porringer
And eat my supper there.'

'The first that died was little Jane;
In bed she moaning lay,
Till God released her of her pain;
And then she went away.

'So in the churchyard she was laid;
And when the grass was dry,
Together round her grave we played,
My brother John and I.

'And when the ground was white with snow
And I could run and slide,
My brother John was forced to go,
And he lies by her side.'

'How many are you then,' said I,
'If they two are in heaven!'
The little maiden did reply,
'Oh master! We are seven!'

'But they are dead; those two are dead!
Their spirits are in heaven!'
'Twas throwing words away: for still
The little maid would have her will
And said, 'Nay, we are seven!'

William Wordsworth, 1770 – 1850

7 Having is a sham (pairs)

In describing Miss Havisham, Dickens paints a picture of a woman who has wealth but not love. Her name is a pun on the phrase, 'having is a sham'.

Use the table below to analyse Miss Havisham's character.

What Miss Havisham was wearing	Evidence of her being frozen in time	Pip's feelings about her
She was dressed in …	She had only one …	She looked like a ghastly …
Her shoes were …	Her veil …	A skeleton …
	Her watch …	I should have …

8 Living in the past (pairs)

Improvise a scene in which Miss Havisham is visited by a counsellor who is trying to help her come to terms with the past and move into the present. You may want to consider the following points:

- **Miss Havisham**
  What is your attitude to Pip and Estella?
  Is it normal to pay one child to amuse another?

- **Counsellor**
  What can you say to help Miss Havisham look to the future?

A Portrait of Miss Havisham

When Pip is still a small child, Miss Havisham, a rich, eccentric lady, employs him as a playmate for her adopted ward, Estella. Miss Havisham was jilted on her wedding day, and although she must be well over 40 now, she remains fixed at a moment in time that was her time of greatest hope and pain.

In an arm-chair, with an elbow resting on the table and her head leaning on that hand, sat the strangest lady I have ever seen, or shall ever see.

She was dressed in rich materials – satins, and lace, and silks, all of white. Her shoes were white. And she had a long white veil dependent from her hair, and she had bridal flowers in her hair, but her hair was white. Some bright jewels sparkled on her neck and on her hands, and some other jewels lay sparkling on the table. Dresses, less splendid than the dress she wore, and half-packed trunks, were scattered about. She had not quite finished dressing, for she had but one shoe on. The other was on the table near her hand. Her veil was but half arranged, her watch and chain were not put on, and some lace for her bosom lay with those trinkets, and with her handkerchief, and gloves, and some flowers, and a Prayer-Book, all confusedly heaped about the looking-glass.

I saw that everything within my view which ought to be white, had been white long ago, and had lost its lustre, and was faded and yellow. I saw that the bride within the bridal dress had withered like the dress, and like the flowers, and had no brightness left but the brightness of her sunken eyes. I saw that the dress had been put upon the rounded figure of a young woman, and that the figure upon which it now hung loose, had shrunk to skin and bone. Once, I had been taken to see some ghastly waxwork at the Fair, representing I know not what impossible personage lying in state. Once, I had been taken to one of our old marsh churches to see a skeleton in the ashes of a rich dress, that had been dug out of a vault under the church pavement. Now waxwork and skeleton seemed to have dark eyes that moved and looked at me. I should have cried out, if I could.

It was when I stood before her, avoiding her eyes, that I took note of the surrounding objects in detail, and saw that her watch had stopped at twenty minutes to nine, and that a clock in the room had stopped at twenty minutes to nine.

'Look at me,' said Miss Havisham. 'You are not afraid of a woman who has never seen the sun since you were born?'

I regret to state that I was not afraid of telling the enormous lie comprehended in the answer, 'No.'

'Do you know what I touch here?' she said, laying her hands, one upon the other, on her left side.

'Yes, ma'am.' (It made me think of the young man.)

'What do I touch?'

'Your heart.'

'Broken!'

9 'Play the game out' (groups of four)

Read and perform the extract opposite. One of you is the narrator and the other three are in role as Miss Havisham, Pip and Estella.

On the second run-through, act the events and add your own words and thoughts as you begin to feel how the characters interact with one another.

10 Estella's feelings (pairs)

- List the words used to describe Estella's manner to Pip. For example, she speaks to him with 'disdain' and she calls him 'boy'. Then explain what each of these words tells you about Estella and her behaviour.

- Would you like to play cards with her? Give your reasons.

11 Social snobbery (pairs)

Copy and complete the chart showing the details of the card game and how Pip and Estella might have thought about it.

Event	Estella's view	Pip's view
Miss Havisham watches the game	'She's watching me to see me put this labouring boy in his place.'	'Estella's frightening me because ... Also, I've never seen anyone so deathly as ....'
A knave is played	'How common! He calls knaves ...'	'I've got it wrong again. What's wrong with what I said?'
	'Pip's hands ...'	

- Write Estella's diary entry describing her card-game with Pip, using the information from your chart. Bring out Estella's snobbery.
- Then write a contrasting diary entry that Pip might have written about the same game. Emphasise Pip's sense of shame.

A Game of Cards

During his first visit to Satis House, Miss Havisham's home, Pip plays a game of cards with Estella but her criticism of him makes him feel uncomfortable.

'I am tired,' said Miss Havisham. 'I want diversion, and I have done with men and women. Play.'

So she sat, corpse-like, as we played at cards; the frillings and trimmings on her bridal dress looking like earthy paper. I knew nothing then of the discoveries that are occasionally made of bodies buried in ancient times, which fall to powder in the moment of being distinctly seen; but I have often thought since, that she must have looked as if the admission of the natural light of day would have struck her to dust.

'He calls the knaves, Jacks, this boy!' said Estella with disdain, before our first game was out. 'And what coarse hands he has. And what thick boots!'

I had never thought of being ashamed of my hands before; but I began to consider them a very indifferent pair. Her contempt was so strong, that it became infectious, and I caught it.

She won the game, and I dealt. I misdealt, as was only natural, when I knew she was lying in wait for me to do wrong; and she denounced me for a stupid, clumsy labouring-boy.

'You say nothing of her,' remarked Miss Havisham to me, as she looked on. 'She says many hard things of you, but you say nothing of her. What do you think of her?'

'I don't like to say,' I stammered.

'Tell me in my ear,' said Miss Havisham, bending down.

'I think she is very proud,' I replied in a whisper.

'Anything else?'

'I think she is very pretty.'

'Anything else?'

'I think she is very insulting.' (She was looking at me then, with a look of supreme aversion.)

'Anything else?'

'I think I should like to go home.'

'And never see her again, though she is so pretty?'

'I am not sure that I shouldn't like to see her again, but I should like to go home now.'

'You shall go soon,' said Miss Havisham aloud. 'Play the game out.'

I played the game to an end with Estella, and she beggared me. She threw the cards down on the table when she had won them all, as if she despised them for having been won of me.

12 My dream (groups of three)

It is normal to feel that you would like a change from home when you grow up. Prepare a presentation about a teenager who wishes he or she could be somewhere else, and who tells family or friends about it.

13 Pip is ashamed of his home (pairs)

Pip's view of his home changes as a result of falling under Estella's influence. Look at these two pictures, then copy and complete the text below. Add examples from the text.

'Home had never been a very pleasant place to me, because of ...'
This suggests that ...

'I had believed in the forge as the glowing road to ...'
This suggests Pip liked his work at the forge because ...

Use your notes to write a paragraph summarising Pip's change in attitude.

14 My expectations (individual)

Write what you would like to be doing in five years' time. This may not mean going anywhere different. It could involve leaving school and doing further study, or getting a job.

CONTINUED ☞

Pip is Ashamed of his Home

Contact with the snobbish Miss Havisham and Estella makes Pip become ashamed of his humble working-class origins and become aware of how society regards the poor and uneducated. He longs to become a gentleman.

It is a most miserable thing to feel ashamed of home. There may be black ingratitude in the thing, and the punishment may be retributive, and well deserved; but, that it is a miserable thing, I can testify.

Home had never been a very pleasant place to me, because of my sister's temper. But Joe had sanctified it, and I had believed in it. I had believed in the best parlour as a most elegant saloon; I had believed in the front door, as a mysterious portal of the Temple of State whose solemn opening was attended with a sacrifice of roast fowls; I had believed in the kitchen as a chaste though not magnificent apartment; I had believed in the forge as the glowing road to manhood and independence. Within a single year, all this was changed. Now, it was all coarse and common, and I would not have had Miss Havisham and Estella see it on any account.

How much of my ungracious condition of mind may have been my own fault, how much Miss Havisham's, how much my sister's, is now of no moment to me or to anyone. The change was made in me; the thing was done. Well or ill done, excusably or inexcusably, it was done.

Once, it had seemed to me that when I should at last roll up my shirt-sleeves and go into the forge, Joe's 'prentice, I should be distinguished and happy. Now the reality was in my hold, I only felt that I was dusty with the dust of small coal, and that I had a weight upon my daily remembrance to which the anvil was a feather. There have been occasions in my later life (I suppose as in most lives) when I have felt for a time as if a thick curtain had fallen on all its interest and romance, to shut me out from anything save dull endurance any more. Never has that curtain dropped so heavy and blank, as when my way lay stretched out straight before me through the newly-entered road of apprenticeship to Joe.

What I wanted, who can say? How can *I* say, when I never knew? What I dreaded was, that in some unlucky hour I, being at my grimiest and commonest, should lift up my eyes and see Estella looking in at one of the wooden windows of the forge. I was haunted by the fear that she would, sooner or later, find me out, with a black face and hands, doing the coarsest part of my work, and would exult over me and despise me.

15 Some amazing news (groups of three or four)

A stranger arrives at your door with exciting news for you and your family. It could be that you have won the lottery or you have found a long-lost relative. Invite the stranger in, and discuss the news.

16 Predictions (individual)

- Use your improvisation and your knowledge of Pip so far to write a prediction about Pip's behaviour and attitude to Joe two years after he hears of his inheritance.
- Write down who you think Pip's benefactor is, and why.

Keep this work safe for a later activity.

Mr Jaggers Brings some Amazing News

Pip grows up and loves Estella but she ignores him. An amazing event happens to Pip. He has just been apprenticed as a blacksmith to Joe Gargery, his brother-in-law, when a lawyer, Mr Jaggers, arrives to tell Pip that he has 'great expectations' (he has inherited money). Pip leaves the marshes for London, believing that his benefactor is Miss Havisham.

It began with the strange gentleman's sitting down at the table, drawing the candle to him, and looking over some entries in his pocket-book. He then put up the pocket-book and set the candle a little aside: after peering round it into the darkness at Joe and me, to ascertain which was which.

'My name', he said, 'is Jaggers, and I am a lawyer in London. I am pretty well known. I have unusual business to transact with you, and I commence by explaining that it is not of my originating. If my advice had been asked, I should not have been here. It was not asked, and you see me here. What I have to do as the confidential agent of another, I do. No less, no more.'

Finding that he could not see us very well from where he sat, he got up, and threw one leg over the back of a chair and leaned upon it; thus having one foot on the seat of the chair, and one foot on the ground.

'Now, Joseph Gargery, I am the bearer of an offer to relieve you of this young fellow, your apprentice. You would not object to cancel his indentures, at his request and for his good? You would want nothing for so doing?'

'The answer is,' returned Joe sternly, 'No.'

'Now, I return to this young fellow. And the communication I have got to make is, that he has Great Expectations.'

Joe and I gasped, and looked at one another.

'I am instructed to communicate to him,' said Mr Jaggers, throwing his finger at me sideways, 'that he will come into a handsome property. Further, that it is the desire of the present possessor of that property, that he be immediately removed from his present sphere of life and from this place, and be brought up as a gentleman – in a word, as a young fellow of great expectations.'

My dream was out; my wild fancy was surpassed by sober reality; Miss Havisham was going to make my fortune on a grand scale.

'Now, Mr Pip,' pursued the lawyer, 'I address the rest of what I have to say, to you. You are to understand, first, that it is the request of the person from whom I take my instructions, that you always bear the name of Pip. You will have no objection, I dare say, to your great expectations being encumbered with that easy condition. But if you have any objection, this is the time to mention it.'

My heart was beating so fast, and there was such a singing in my ears, that I could scarcely stammer I had no objection.

'I should think not! Now you are to understand, secondly, Mr Pip, that the name of the person who is your liberal benefactor remains a profound secret, until the person chooses to reveal it.'

An Unexpected Visitor

Pip is now in his twenties and studying in London for a law degree. One stormy night, he is working alone in his chambers, when he has an unexpected visitor. The stranger reveals that he is Magwitch, the escaped convict who forced Pip to help him at the beginning of the story. Magwitch prospered in Australia, after being transported there as a criminal. He returned to Britain in order to contact Pip.

I read with my watch upon the table, purposing to close my book at eleven o'clock. As I shut it, Saint Paul's, and all the many church-clocks in the City – some leading, some accompanying, some following – struck that hour. The sound was curiously flawed by the wind; and I was listening, and thinking how the wind assailed and tore it, when I heard a footstep on the stair.

I stood with my lamp held out over the stair-rail, and he came slowly within its light. I made out that he was substantially dressed, but roughly; like a voyager by sea. That he had long iron-gray hair. That his age was about sixty. That he was a muscular man, strong on his legs, and that he was browned and hardened by exposure to weather. As he ascended the last stair or two, and the light of my lamp included us both, I saw, with a stupid kind of amazement, that he was holding out both his hands to me.

'Pray, what is your business?' I asked him.

'My business?' he repeated, pausing. 'Ah! Yes. I will explain my business, by your leave.'

'Do you wish to come in?'

'Yes', he replied; 'I wish to come in, Master.'

I had asked the question inhospitably enough, for I resented the sort of bright and gratified recognition that still shone in his face. I resented it, because it seemed to imply that he expected me to respond to it. But I took him into the room I had just left, and, having set the lamp on the table, asked him as civilly as I could, to explain himself.

He looked about him with the strangest air – an air of wondering pleasure, as if he had some part in the things he admired – and he pulled off a rough outer coat, and his hat. Then, I saw that his head was furrowed and bald, and that the long iron-gray hair grew only on its sides. But I saw nothing that in the least explained him. On the contrary, I saw him next moment, once more holding out both his hands to me.

'What do you mean?' said I, half suspecting him to be mad.

He stopped in his looking at me, and slowly rubbed his right hand over his head. 'It's disappointing to a man', he said, in a coarse, broken voice, 'arter having looked for'ard so distant, and come so fur; but you're not to blame for that – neither on us is to blame for that. I'll speak in half a minute. Give me half a minute, please.'

He sat down on a chair that stood before the fire, and covered his forehead with his large brown veinous hands. I looked at him attentively then, and recoiled a little from him; but I did not know him.

CONTINUED ☞

17 Pip and the stranger (pairs)

Dickens gives the strange visitor speech patterns that are quite different from Pip's. Make a chart comparing the two different ways of speaking, or *registers*.

The stranger's speech patterns	Pip's speech patterns
'by your leave'	'Pray, what is your business'
'I wish to come in ...'	'Do you wish ...'
' arter having looked for'ard ...'	
'neither on us ...'	

What conclusions can you draw from their speech about:
- how well they are educated
- how well they know one another
- Pip's attitude to the stranger and the stranger's attitude to Pip?

Draft and present to the class a conversation between two people who speak quite differently from one another. Make sure you include different vocabulary, not just different accents.

18 Opposite reactions (pairs)

Dickens makes it clear that Pip and Magwitch react differently to this meeting. Use the diagram below to analyse how Dickens shows Pip's horror and Magwitch's pleasure.

Character	What he says	How he reacts	Dickens' language
Pip	When asked if he thought his benefactor was Magwitch, he replied ...		Repetition of '... and exclamation' shows
Magwitch	'Pip dear boy' shows he knows him and is fond of him. 'You're my son' shows ...	He takes hold of both Pip's hands. This shows ...	Repetition of 'dear boy' shows ...

An Unexpected Visitor (continued)

'There's no one nigh,' said he, looking over his shoulder, 'is there?'

'Why do you, a stranger coming into my rooms at this time of the night, ask that question?' said I.

... 'Pip, dear boy, I've made a gentleman on you! It's me wot has done it! I swore that time, sure as ever I earned a guinea, that guinea should go to you. I swore arterwards, sure as ever I spec'lated and got rich, you should get rich. I lived rough, that you should live smooth; I worked hard that you should be above work. What odds, dear boy? Do I tell it fur you to feel a obligation? Not a bit. I tell it, fur you to know as that there hunted dunghill dog wot you kep life in, got his head so high that he could make a gentleman and, Pip, you're him!'

The abhorrence in which I held the man, the dread I had of him, the repugnance with which I shrank from him, could not have been exceeded if he had been some terrible beast.

'Look'ee here, Pip. I'm your second father. You're my son — more to me nor any son. I've put away money, only for you to spend. When I was a hired-out shepherd in a solitary hut, not seeing no faces but faces of sheep till I half forgot wot men's and women's faces was like, I see yourn. I drops my knife many a time in that hut when I was a-eating my dinner or my supper, and I says, "Here's the boy again, a-looking at me whiles I eats and drinks!" I see you there a-many times as plain as ever I see you on them misty marshes. "Lord strike me dead!" I says each time – and I goes out in the air to say it under the open heavens – "but wot, if I gets liberty and money, I'll make that boy a gentleman!" And I done it. Why, look at you, dear boy! Look at these here lodgings of yourn, fit for a lord! A lord? Ah! You shall show money with lords for wagers, and beat 'em!'

In his heat and triumph, and in his knowledge that I had been nearly fainting, he did not remark on my reception of all this. It was the one grain of relief I had.

'Look at your linen; fine and beautiful! Look at your clothes; better ain't to be got! And your books too,' turning his eyes round the room, 'mounting up, on their shelves, by hundreds! And you read 'em; don't you? I see you'd been a reading of 'em when I come in. Ha, ha, ha! You shall read 'em to me, dear boy! And if they're in foreign languages wot I don't understand, I shall be just as proud as if I did.'

He took both my hands and put them to his lips, while my blood ran cold within me.

'Don't you mind talking, Pip,' said he.

'You ain't looked slowly forward to this as I have; you wosn't prepared for this, as I wos. But didn't you never think it might be me?'

'Oh no, no, no,' I returned. 'Never, never!'

'Well, you see it *was* me, and single-handed. Never a soul in it but my own self and Mr Jaggers.'

'Was there no one else?' I asked.

'No,' said he, with a glance of surprise: 'who else should there be?'

Magwitch's Escape Bid

Pip gradually becomes sympathetic to Magwitch. He and two friends, Herbert and Startop, try to smuggle Magwitch out of Harwich in a rowing boat and aboard a steamer to Hamburg but the plan goes wrong and they are caught by the customs men.

We got aboard the rowing boat easily, and rowed out into the track of the steamer. By that time it wanted but ten minutes of one o'clock, and we began to look out for her smoke.

But it was half-past one before we saw her smoke, and soon afterwards we saw behind it the smoke of another steamer. As they were coming on at full speed, we got the two bags ready, and took that opportunity of saying good-bye to Herbert and Startop. We had all shaken hands cordially, and neither Herbert's eyes nor mine were quite dry, when I saw a four-oared galley shoot out from under the bank but a little way ahead of us, and row out into the same track.

A stretch of shore had been as yet between us and the steamer's smoke, by reason of the bend and wind of the river, but now she was visible, coming head on. I called to Herbert and Startop to keep before the tide, that she might see us lying by for her, and I adjured Magwitch to sit quite still, wrapped in his cloak. He answered cheerily, 'Trust to me, dear boy,' and sat like a statue. Meantime the galley, which was skilfully handled, had crossed us, let us come up with her, and fallen alongside. Leaving just room enough for the play of the oars, she kept alongside, drifting when we drifted, and pulling a stroke or two when we pulled. Of the two sitters, one held the rudder lines, and looked at us attentively– as did all the rowers; the other sitter was wrapped up, much as Magwitch was, and seemed to shrink, and whisper some instruction to the steerer as he looked at us. Not a word was spoken in either boat.

Startop could make out, after a few minutes, which steamer was first, and gave me the word 'Hamburg', in a low voice as we sat face to face. She was nearing us very fast, and the beating of her paddles grew louder and louder. I felt as if her shadow were absolutely upon us, when the galley hailed us. I answered.

'You have a returned transport there,' said the man who held the lines. 'That's the man, wrapped in the cloak. His name is Abel Magwitch. I apprehend that man, and call upon him to surrender, and you to assist.'

At the same moment, without giving any audible direction to his crew, he ran the galley aboard of us. They had pulled one sudden stroke ahead, had got their oars in, had run athwart us, and were holding on to our gunwale, before we knew what they were doing. This caused great confusion on board the steamer, and I heard them calling to us, and heard the order given to stop the paddles, and heard them stop, but felt her driving down upon us irresistibly. In the same moment, I saw the steersman of the galley lay his hand on his prisoner's shoulder, and saw that both boats were swinging round with the force of the tide, and saw that all hands on board the steamer were running forward quite frantically.

Magwitch's Escape Bid (continued)

I heard a great cry on board the steamer and a loud splash in the water, and felt the boat sink from under me.

It was but for an instant that I seemed to struggle with a thousand mill-weirs and a thousand flashes of light; that instant past, I was taken on board the galley. Herbert was there, and Startop was there; but our boat was gone, and the two convicts were gone.

What with the cries aboard the steamer, and the furious blowing-off of her steam, and her driving on, and our driving on, I could not at first distinguish sky from water or shore from shore; but the crew of the galley righted her with great speed, and pulling certain swift, strong strokes ahead, lay upon their oars, every man looking silently and eagerly at the water astern. Presently a dark object was seen in it, bearing towards us on the tide. No man spoke, but the steersman held up his hand, and all softly backed water, and kept the boat straight and true before it. As it came nearer, I saw it to be Magwitch, swimming, but not swimming freely. He was taken on board, and instantly manacled at the wrists and ankles.

The galley was kept steady, and the silent, eager look-out at the water was resumed. But the Rotterdam steamer now came up, and apparently, not understanding what had happened, came on at speed. By the time she had been hailed and stopped, both steamers were drifting away from us, and we were rising and falling in a troubled wake of water. The look-out was kept, long after all was still again and the two steamers were gone; but everybody knew that it was hopeless now.

CONTINUED ☞

19 Predictions (groups of three)

Pip has gradually become more sympathetic to Magwitch, the convict who became his benefactor, as he has grown up and understands him more.

- Make a list of the mistakes Pip has made as he looks back on his life – his snobbery, his desire to escape from his home, and his ingratitude to Joe.
- Improvise the scene where he returns and apologises to Joe, who is now married to a motherly woman called Biddy (Pip's sister died many years ago).

20 Magwitch's bid to escape (drafting in pairs)

List the events leading to Magwitch's re-capture. Discuss how the story would have been reported in the newspapers. Think about:

- whose side the reporter would be on
- the type of headlines and interviews that would be featured
- the pictures and captions that would be used.

Draft your ideas, and write a newspaper article.

21 A tale with a twist (individual)

Plan and write your own tale with a twist. Tell it in the first person, as if the events are happening to you. Use *pathetic fallacy* (see page 78) and *peripeteia* (sudden change of fortune) to give your story depth and excitement.

Magwitch's Escape Bid (continued)

At length we gave it up, and pulled under the shore towards the tavern we had lately left, where we were received with no little surprise. Here, I was able to get some comforts for Magwitch who had received some very severe injury in the chest and a deep cut in the head.

He told me that he believed himself to have gone under the keel of the steamer, and to have been struck on the head in rising. The injury to his chest (which rendered his breathing extremely painful) he thought he had received against the side of the galley. He added that he did not pretend to say what he might or might not have done to Compeyson, but that in the moment of his laying his hand on his cloak to identify him, that villain had staggered up and staggered back, and they had both gone overboard together; when the sudden wrenching of him (Magwitch) out of our boat, and the endeavour of his captor to keep him in it, had capsized us. He told me in a whisper that they had gone down, fiercely locked in each others' arms, and that there had been a struggle under water, and that he had disengaged himself, struck out, and swum away.

I never had any reason to doubt the exact truth of what he had told me. The officer who steered the galley gave the same account of their going overboard.

When I asked this officer's permission to change the prisoner's wet clothes by purchasing any spare garments I could get at the public-house, he gave it readily: merely observing that he must take charge of everything the prisoner had about him. So the pocket-book which had once been in my hands, passed into the officer's. He further gave me leave to accompany the prisoner to London; but declined to accord that grace to my two friends.

The Jack at the Ship was instructed where the drowned man had gone down, and undertook to search for the body in the places where it was likeliest to come ashore. His interest in its recovery seemed to me to be much heightened when he heard that it had stockings on. Probably, it took about a dozen drowned men to fit him out completely; and that may have been the reason why the different articles of his dress were in various stages of decay.

We remained at the public-house until the tide turned, and then Magwitch was carried down to the galley and put on board. Herbert and Startop were to get to London by land, as soon as they could. We had a doleful parting, and when I took my place by Magwitch's side, I felt that that was my place henceforth while he lived.

For now my repugnance to him had all melted away, and in the hunted, wounded, shackled creature who held my hand in his, I only saw a man who had meant to be my benefactor, and who had felt affectionately, gratefully, and generously towards me with great constancy throughout a series of years. I only saw in him a much better man than I had been to Joe.

A TALE OF TWO CITIES

A Swashbuckling Yarn

1 A marriage made in Heaven/Hell (pairs)

Imagine you are two friends who know a couple about to get married. One sees the positive side, the other the negative side. Prepare a scene where you each give short opinions that the other contradicts.

For example:

Person A   *Two can live as cheaply as one*
Person B   *Not with the amount they both spend!*

2 A sense of perspective (individual)

The opening of a novel normally sets the scene, introduces characters and gives the reader a sense of perspective on events about to unfold. Dickens' novel is set during the French Revolution, a time of war when sometimes friends were fighting on opposite sides. At such a time it was difficult to make clear judgements about what was right and wrong. That is why Dickens uses *antithesis* (opposites) at the beginning of *A Tale of Two Cities*.

List the opposites in the first paragraph, then choose two of them to explain to the class.

the best of times	*the worst of times*
age of wisdom	*age of foolishness*
epoch of belief	
season of Light	

- Write the opening of a novel set in your school or home-town, using antithesis.

3 France and England (pairs)

Look closely at what Dickens writes about France and England. Make notes on what he is saying about each society.

Then read out two or three antitheses that summarise Dickens' ideas about the two countries.

The Grand Perspective

Dickens introduces this novel with a survey of the social turmoil in England and France just before the start of the French Revolution.

It was the best of times, it was the worst of times, it was the age of wisdom, it was the age of foolishness, it was the epoch of belief, it was the epoch of incredulity, it was the season of Light, it was the season of Darkness, it was the spring of hope, it was the winter of despair, we had everything before us, we had nothing before us, we were all going direct to Heaven, we were all going direct the other way – in short, the period was so far like the present period, that some of its noisiest authorities insisted on its being received, for good or for evil, in the superlative degree of comparison only.

There were a king with a large jaw and a queen with a plain face, on the throne of England; there were a king with a large jaw and a queen with a fair face, on the throne of France. In both countries it was clearer than crystal to the lords of the State preserves of loaves and fishes, that things in general were settled for ever.

It was the year of Our Lord one thousand seven hundred and seventy five. France rolled with exceeding smoothness downhill, making paper money and spending it. Under the guidance of her Christian pastors, she entertained herself, besides, with such humane achievements as sentencing a youth to have his hands cut off, his tongue torn out with pincers, and his body burned alive, because he had not kneeled down in the rain to do honour to a dirty procession of monks which passed within his view.

In England, there was scarcely an amount of order and protection to justify much national boasting. Daring burglaries by armed men, and highway robberies, took place in the capital itself every night; families were publicly cautioned not to go out of town without removing their furniture to warehouses for security; the mail was waylaid by seven robbers, and the guard shot three dead, and then got shot dead himself by the other four, after which the mail was robbed in peace; prisoners in London gaols fought battles with their turnkeys; thieves snipped off diamond crosses from the necks of noble lords at Court drawing-rooms. In the midst of them, the hangman, ever busy and ever worse than useless, was in constant requisition, now stringing up long rows of miscellaneous criminals, now, a wretched pilferer who had robbed a farmer's boy of sixpence.

An Incident on the Stagecoach

Dickens opens A Tale of Two Cities *in an atmosphere of mystery and suspense.*
Mr Lorry, who is travelling to Dover on the night mail-coach, receives a mysterious
message from the bank he works for.

It was the Dover road that lay, on a Friday night late in November, before the first of
the persons with whom this history has business. He walked uphill in the mire by the
side of the mail, as the rest of the passengers did; not because they had the least
relish for walking exercise, under the circumstances, but because the hill, and the
harness, and the mud, and the mail, were all so heavy, that the horses had three
times already come to a stop, besides once drawing the coach across the road, with
the mutinous intent of taking it back to Blackheath.

Two other passengers, besides the one, were plodding up the hill by the side of the
mail. All three were wrapped to the cheek-bones and over the ears, and wore jack-
boots. Not one of the three could have said, from anything he saw, what either of the
other two was like; and each was hidden under almost as many wrappers from the
eyes of the mind, as from the eyes of the body, of his two companions. In those days,
travellers were very shy of being confidential on a short notice, for anybody on the
road might be a robber or in league with robbers.

'Wo-ho!' said the coachman. 'So, then! One more pull and you're at the top and be
damned to you, for I have had trouble enough to get you to it! – Joe!'

'Halloa!' the guard replied.

'What o'clock do you make it, Joe?'

'Ten minutes, good, past eleven.'

'My blood!' exclaimed the vexed coachman, 'and not atop of Shooter's Hill yet!
Tst! Yah! Get on with you!'

The last burst carried the mail to the summit of the hill. The horses stopped to
breathe again, and the guard got down to skid the wheel for the descent, and open
the coach-door to let the passengers in.

'Tst! Joe!' cried the coachman in a warning voice, looking down from his box.

'What do you say, Tom?'

They both listened.

'I say a horse at a canter coming up, Joe.'

'*I* say a horse at a gallop, Tom,' returned the guard, leaving his hold of the door,
and mounting nimbly to his place. 'Gentlemen! In the king's name, all of you!'

The sound of a horse at a gallop came fast and furiously up the hill.

'So-ho!' the guard sang out, as loud as he could roar. 'Yo there! Stand! I shall fire!'

The pace was suddenly checked, and, with much splashing and floundering, a
man's voice called from the mist, 'Is that the Dover mail?'

'Never you mind what it is!' the guard retorted. 'What are you?'

'*Is* that the Dover mail?'

'Why do you want to know?'

CONTINUED ☞

4 Mysterious messages (pairs)

This is an activity in two parts:

(a) Write a five-word instruction on a piece of paper.

(b) Swap with another pair and improvise a scene around the instructions.

5 The start of an adventure (pairs)

Adventure stories use a range of conventions to engage the reader's attention. Copy and complete the chart below to explore some of the conventions Dickens uses at the beginning of *A Tale of Two Cities*.

Conventions of adventure story	Evidence at opening	Effect on reader
Characters: dynamic – there is a hero in conflict with enemies	Not enough evidence that Mr Lorry is the hero. He is employed by the Bank and may be a way into the story.	Intriguing; leaves us wondering ...
Plot: unexpected events		
Setting: dramatic and varied	Winter night, darkness, anonymous people. Difficult journey up Shooter's Hill.	
Atmosphere: unease and tension		

6 Predictions (pairs)

Using evidence from 'An Incident on the Stagecoach', make predictions about what might happen in the story.

An Incident on the Stagecoach (continued)

'I want a passenger, if it is.'

'What passenger?'

'Mr Jarvis Lorry.'

Our booked passenger showed in a moment that it was his name. The guard, the coachman, and the two other passengers eyed him distrustfully.

'Keep where you are,' the guard called to the voice in the mist, 'because, if I should make a mistake, it could never be set right in your lifetime. Gentleman of the name of Lorry answer straight.'

'What is the matter?' asked the passenger, then, with mildly quavering speech. 'Who wants me? Is it Jerry?'

('I don't like Jerry's voice, if it is Jerry,' growled the guard to himself. 'He's hoarser than suits me, is Jerry.')

'Yes, Mr Lorry.'

'What is the matter?'

'A despatch sent you from over yonder. T. and Co.'

'I know this messenger, guard,' said Mr Lorry, getting down into the road – assisted from behind more swiftly than politely by the other two passengers, who immediately scrambled into the coach, shut the door, and pulled up the window. 'He may come close; there's nothing wrong.'

The watchful guard, with his right hand at the stock of his raised blunderbuss, his left at the barrel, and his eye on the horseman, answered curtly, 'Sir.'

'There is nothing to apprehend. I belong to Tellson's Bank. You must know Tellson's Bank in London. I am going to Paris on business. A crown to drink. I may read this?'

'If so be as you're quick, sir.'

He opened it in the light of the coach-lamp on that side and read – first to himself and then aloud: '"Wait – at Dover for Mam'selle," It's not long, you see, guard. Jerry, say that my answer was, RECALLED TO LIFE.'

Linked Text

7 Poetry reading (groups of four)

Work together to prepare a dramatic reading of 'The Highwayman'. Pay particular attention to:

- *rhythm*   the number of strong beats in a line
- *rhyme*   how couplets (pairs of rhymes) work together
- *punctuation*   this gives clues about the pace of the poem.

8 Alliteration in the poem (pairs)

Alliteration is where two or more words near each other are linked by starting with the same sound:

'The road was a ribbon of moonlight over the purple moor'

Find other examples of alliteration in the poem and add them to a copy of this table.

Line using alliteration	Pictures created	Effect of alliteration
The road was a ribbon of moonlight over the purple moor		Emphasises winding feel of the road, slightly glistening.
		The beautiful, mysterious colour of the heather on the moor emphasised.
Dumb as a dog he listened		

9 The sound of a horse at a gallop (pairs)

Why do the guard and passengers in 'An Incident on the Stagecoach' feel nervous when they hear hoofs on the road behind them?

The Highwayman

The first thing that passengers on a stagecoach would think when hailed by a lone horseman at nearly midnight, was that a highwayman was approaching to rob and perhaps kill them. Here is a linked text for you to read.

The wind was a torrent of darkness among the gusty trees,
The moon was a ghostly galleon tossed upon cloudy seas,
The road was a ribbon of moonlight over the purple moor,
And the highwayman came riding –
       Riding – riding –
The highwayman came riding, up to the old inn-door.

He'd a French cocked-hat on his forehead, a bunch of lace at his chin,
A coat of the claret velvet, and breeches of brown doeskin:
They fitted with never a wrinkle; his boots were up to the thigh!
And he rode with a jewelled twinkle,
       His pistol butts a-twinkle,
His rapier hilt a-twinkle, under the jewelled sky.

Over the cobbles he clattered and clashed in the dark inn-yard,
And he tapped with his whip on the shutters, but all was locked and barred:
He whistled a tune to the window; and who should be waiting there
But the landlord's black-eyed daughter,
       Bess, the landlord's daughter,
Plaiting a dark red love-knot into her long black hair.

And dark in the dark old inn-yard a stable-wicket creaked
Where Tim, the ostler, listened; his face was white and peaked,
His eyes were hollows of madness, his hair like mouldy hay;
But he loved the landlord's daughter,
       The landlord's red-lipped daughter:
Dumb as a dog he listened, and he heard the robber say –

'One kiss, my bonny sweetheart, I'm after a prize tonight,
But I shall be back with the yellow gold before the
    morning light.
Yet if they press me sharply, and harry me through
    the day,
       Then look for me by moonlight,
              Watch for me by moonlight:
       I'll come to thee by moonlight, though
              Hell should bar the way.'

Alfred Noyes, 1880 – 1958

10 Triggering memories (pairs)

Improvise a scene where one of you hands the other an object (real or imaginary) that triggers a memory. This memory could be about a person, place or event. Share your memories then swap roles.

11 'Recalled to life' (individual)

Dr Manette is in a state of shock and has lost his memory as a result of his experiences in prison, where he passed his time making shoes. To begin with, he does not recognise either his daughter or Mr Lorry.

Write a first-person account of the thoughts that go through his mind as he realises who his visitors are. The following beginning may help:

I was working hard at my last* making a new pair of shoes. The leather was tough and I was concentrating, as I didn't want to spoil the shoes. I suddenly became aware of a man standing close beside me. I was surprised, but I didn't speak …

* Last: an upright iron shape in the form of a foot used for making shoes.

Dr Manette Recalled to Life

Mr Lorry followed the instructions in his note from the Bank, and met Lucie Manette at Dover. They travelled together to Paris, where they found her father Dr Manette ('recalled to life') who had been rescued from prison by the citizens and hidden by his old servants, the Defarges.

Mr Lorry came silently forward, leaving Lucie by the door. When he had stood, for a minute or two, by the side of Defarge, the shoemaker looked up. He showed no surprise at seeing another figure.

'You have a visitor, you see,' said Monsieur Defarge.

'You are not a shoemaker by trade?' said Mr Lorry, looking steadfastly at the shoemaker.

His haggard eyes turned to Mr Lorry. 'I am not a shoemaker by trade? No, I was not a shoemaker by trade. I – I learnt it here. I taught myself. I asked leave to –'

He started, and resumed, in the manner of a sleeper that moment awake, reverting to a subject of last night.

'I asked leave to teach myself, and I got it with much difficulty after a long while, and I have made shoes ever since.'

As he held out his hand for the shoe that had been taken from him, Mr Lorry said, still looking steadfastly in his face:

'Monsieur Manette, do you remember nothing of me?'

The shoe dropped to the ground, and he sat looking fixedly at the questioner.

Not a word was spoken, not a sound was made. Lucie stood, like a spirit, beside him, and he bent over his work.

'You are not the gaoler's daughter?'

She sighed, 'No.'

'Who are you?'

Not yet trusting the tones of her voice, she sat down on the bench beside him. He recoiled, but she laid her hand upon his arm. A strange thrill struck him when she did so, and visibly passed over his frame; he laid the knife down softly, as he sat staring at her.

Her golden hair, which she wore in long curls, had been hurriedly pushed aside, and fell down over her neck. Advancing his hand by little and little, he took it up and looked at it. In the midst of the action he went astray, and, with another deep sigh, fell to work at his shoemaking.

But not for long. Releasing his arm, she laid her hand upon his shoulder. After looking doubtfully at it, two or three times, as if to be sure that it was really there, he laid down his work, put his hand to his neck, and took off a blackened string with a scrap of folded rag attached to it. He opened this, carefully, on his knee, and it contained a very little quantity of hair: not more than one or two long golden hairs, which he had, in some old day, wound upon his finger.

He took her hair into his hand again, and looked closely at it. 'It is the same. How can it be! When was it! How was it!'

As the concentrating expression returned to his forehead, he seemed to become conscious that it was in hers too. He turned her full to the light, and looked at her.

12 The aristocracy (pairs)

Dickens creates a vivid picture of the Marquis in this passage. Look carefully at how our impression of him develops as the extract unfolds. Create a chart like this one.

	What the Marquis looks like; words used to describe him	What he says and does	Our impression of him
Beginning of the passage	'a man of about sixty, handsomely dressed'	He walked quietly down the stairs after shaking the snuff from his fingers	Creates an image of an educated, refined, civilised man.
Middle of the passage		'What has gone wrong?' said Monsieur, calmly looking out.	
End of the passage			

Using the information you have listed, and your own interpretation, write a paragraph explaining how our understanding of the character of the Marquis changes through the passage.

13 The common people (groups of three)

Show how the people observing the scene react, by completing the following:

- Write the thoughts of three different observers, e.g. the father, the ragged and submissive man, the Marquis.
- Draw two pictures of the scene. To these add captions and thought sections in which you make the action and the reaction of the characters clear.

The Marquis

We are still in France. In this short scene Dickens creates a chilling picture of the Marquis, a member of the French aristocracy.

'I devote you,' said this person, stopping at the last door on his way, and turning in the direction of the sanctuary, 'to the Devil!'

With that, he shook the snuff from his fingers as if he had shaken the dust from his feet, and quietly walked downstairs.

He was a man of about sixty, handsomely dressed, haughty in manner, and with a face like a fine mask. A face of a transparent paleness; every feature in it clearly defined; one set expression on it. The nose, beautifully formed otherwise, was very slightly pinched at the top of each nostril. It was a handsome face, and a remarkable one.

Its owner went downstairs into the courtyard, got into his carriage, and drove away.

With a wild rattle and clatter, and an inhuman abandonment of consideration not easy to be understood in these days, the carriage dashed through streets and swept round corners, with women screaming before it, and men clutching each other and clutching children out of its way. At last, swooping at a street corner by a fountain, one of its wheels came to a sickening little jolt, and there was a loud cry from a number of voices, and the horses reared and plunged.

But for the latter inconvenience, the carriage probably would not have stopped; carriages were often known to drive on, and leave their wounded behind, and why not? But the frightened valet had got down in a hurry, and there were twenty hands at the horses' bridles.

'What has gone wrong?' said Monsieur, calmly looking out.

A tall man in a nightcap had caught up a bundle from among the feet of the horses, and had laid it on the basement of the fountain, and was down in the mud and wet, howling over it like a wild animal.

'Pardon, Monsieur the Marquis!' said a ragged and submissive man, 'it is a child.'

'Why does he make that abominable noise? Is it his child?'

'Excuse me, Monsieur the Marquis – it is a pity – yes.'

'Killed!' shrieked the man, in wild desperation, extending both arms at their length above his head, and staring at him, 'Dead!'

The people closed round, and looked at Monsieur the Marquis. There was nothing revealed by the many eyes that looked at him but watchfulness and eagerness; there was no visible menacing or anger. Neither did the people say anything; after the first cry, they had been silent, and they remained so. Monsieur the Marquis ran his eyes over them all, as if they had been mere rats come out of their holes.

He took out his purse.

'It is extraordinary to me,' said he, 'that you people cannot take care of yourselves and your children. One or the other of you is for ever in the way. How do I know what injury you have done my horses? See! Give him that.'

14 Radio play (pairs)

Charles Darnay, a refugee from the French Revolution, has been saved from
a charge of treason by Sydney Carton, a hard-drinking lawyer. Sydney points
out the incredible likeness between himself and Charles Darnay. Both men
fall in love with Lucie Manette.

Prepare a reading of the passage suitable for radio. Consider how to create
atmosphere through the pace of reading, sound effects and dialogue.

15 What happens next? (pairs)

Look carefully at the way the passage is written, in terms of sentence
structure, tone and dialogue. Imagine how the conversation between Dr
Manette and Charles Darnay progresses, and how Dr Manette reacts to
Charles Darnay's request to marry his daughter.

Charles Darnay Asks for Lucie's Hand

Mr Lorry and Lucie return to London with Dr Manette. They meet a young Frenchman called Charles Darnay. He and Lucie fall in love. He asks her father for her hand in marriage.

In London, Charles had expected neither to walk on pavements of gold, nor to lie on beds of roses: if he had had any such exalted expectation, he would not have prospered. He had expected labour, and he found it, and did it, and made the best of it. In this, his prosperity consisted.

He had loved Lucie Manette from the hour of his danger. He had never heard a sound so sweet and dear as the sound of her compassionate voice; he had never seen a face so tenderly beautiful, as hers when it was confronted with his own. But he had never yet, by so much as a single spoken word, disclosed to her the state of his heart.

That he had his reasons for this, he knew full well. It was again a summer day when, lately arrived in London from his college occupation, he turned into the quiet corner in Soho, bent on seeking an opportunity of opening his mind to Doctor Manette. It was the close of the summer day and he knew Lucie to be out.

He found the Doctor reading in his armchair at a window. The energy which had at once supported him under his old sufferings and aggravated their sharpness, had been gradually restored to him. He was now a very energetic man indeed, with great firmness of purpose, strength of resolution and vigour of action.

He studied much, slept little, sustained a great deal of fatigue with ease, and was equally cheerful. To him, now entered Charles Darnay, at sight of whom he laid aside his book and held out his hand.

'Charles Darnay! I rejoice to see you. We have been counting on your return these three or four days past. Mr Stryver and Sydney Carton were both here yesterday, and both made you out to be more than due.'

'I am obliged to them for their interest in the matter,' he answered, a little coldly as to them, though very warmly as to the Doctor. 'Miss Manette –'

'Is well,' said the Doctor, as he stopped short, 'and your return will delight us all She has gone out on some household matters, but will soon be home.'

'Doctor Manette, I knew she was from home, I took the opportunity of her being from home, to beg to speak to you.'

There was a blank silence.

'Yes?' said the Doctor, with evident constraint, 'Bring your chair here, and speak on.'

16 Self-esteem (groups of three)

We all have failings, but the way that Sydney talks about himself shows his low self-esteem.

Imagine an interview situation. Two of you are applying for the same job. One of you has low self-esteem and the other has more confidence. Improvise the scenes when the two of you meet outside, and then during the interviews.

17 Society's conventions (pairs)

In Victorian times it was usual for a man to approach his chosen lady's father and formally ask him for her hand in marriage. Examine the behaviour of Charles Darnay on page 111 and that of Sydney Carton. What can you establish about the character of each man?

18 Victorian emotions (pairs)

The way that Sydney and Lucie talk to each other about their emotions is typical of a Victorian novel. Use the chart below to find evidence of this.

Expressions of emotions in Victorian novels	Examples from *A Tale of Two Cities*
Long, multiple sentences (phrases linked by commas or 'and')	
Formal language	Sydney calls Lucie 'Miss Manette'
Hyperbole (over-the-top expressions)	

Sydney Carton Tells Lucie He Loves Her

Sydney Carton, a young English lawyer, has realised that he is in love with Lucie. He knows that the hard-drinking, reckless life he leads would not make him a fit husband for her, and that she loves Charles Darnay. He lets her know his feelings and promises that he will do anything in his power to ensure her happiness.

He was shown upstairs, and found Lucie at her work, alone. She had never been quite at her ease with him, and received him with some little embarrassment as he seated himself near her table. But, looking up at his face in the interchange of the first few common-places, she observed a change in it.

'I fear you are not well, Mr Carton!'

'No. But the life I lead, Miss Manette, is not conducive to health. What is to be expected of, or by, such profligates?'

'Is it not – forgive me; I have begun the question on my lips – a pity to live no better life?'

'God knows it is a shame!'

'Then why not change it?'

Looking gently at him again, she was surprised and saddened to see that there were tears in his eyes. There were tears in his voice too, as he answered:

'It is too late for that. I shall never be better than I am. I shall sink lower, and be worse.'

He leaned an elbow on her table, and covered his eyes with his hand. The table trembled in the silence that followed.

She had never seen him softened, and was much distressed. He knew her to be so, without looking at her, and said:

'Pray forgive me, Miss Manette. I break down before the knowledge of what I want to say to you. Will you hear me?'

'If it will do you any good, Mr Carton, if it would make you happier, it would make me very glad!'

'God bless you for your sweet compassion!'

He unshaded his face after a little while, and spoke steadily.

'Don't be afraid to hear me. Don't shrink from anything I say. I am like one who died young. All my life might have been.'

'If it has been possible, Miss Manette, that you could have returned the love of the man you see before you – self-flung away, wasted, drunken, poor creature of misuse as you know him to be – he would have been conscious this day and hour, in spite of his happiness, that he would bring you to misery, bring you to sorrow and repentance, blight you, disgrace you, pull you down with him. I know very well that you can have no tenderness for me; I ask for none; I am even thankful that it cannot be.'

'Without it, can I not save you, Mr Carton? Can I not recall you – forgive me again! – to a better course? Can I in no way repay your confidence? I know this is a

CONTINUED ☞

Sydney Carton Tells Lucie He Loves Her (continued)

confidence,' she modestly said, after a little hesitation, and in earnest tears, 'I know you would say this to no one else. Can I turn it to no good account for yourself, Mr Carton?'

He shook his head.

'To none. No, Miss Manette, to none. If you will hear me through a very little more, all you can ever do for me is done. I wish you to know that you have been the last dream of my soul. In my degradation I have not been so degraded but that the sight of you with your father, and of this home made such a home by you, has stirred old shadows that I thought had died out of me. Since I knew you, I have been troubled by a remorse that I thought would never reproach me again, and have heard whispers from old voices impelling me upward, that I thought were silent for ever. I have had unformed ideas of striving afresh, beginning anew, shaking off sloth and sensuality, and fighting out the abandoned fight. A dream, all a dream, that ends in nothing, and leaves the sleeper where he lay down, but I wish you to know that you inspired it.'

'Will nothing of it remain? O Mr Carton, think again! Try again!'

'No, Miss Manette; all through it, I have known myself to be quite undeserving. And yet I have had the weakness, and have still the weakness, to wish you to know with what a sudden mastery you kindled me, heap of ashes that I am, into fire – a fire, however, inseparable in its nature from myself; quickening nothing, lighting nothing, doing no service, idly burning away.'

'The utmost good that I am capable of now, Miss Manette, I have come here to realise. Let me carry through the rest of my misdirected life, the remembrance that I opened my heart to you, last of all the world; and that there was something left in me at this time which you could deplore and pity.'

'Which I entreated you to believe, again and again, most fervently, with all my heart, was capable of better things, Mr Carton!'

'Entreat me to believe it no more, Miss Manette. I have proved myself, and I know better. I distress you; I draw fast to an end. Will you let me believe, when I recall this day, that the last confidence of my life was reposed in your pure and innocent breast, and that it lies there alone, and will be shared by no one?'

'If that will be a consolation to you, yes.'

'Not even by the dearest one ever to be known to you?'

'Mr Carton,' she answered, after an agitated pause, 'the secret is yours, not mine; and I promise to respect it.'

'Thank you. And again, God bless you.'

He put her hand to his lips, and moved towards the door.

'Be under no apprehension, Miss Manette, of my ever resuming this conversation by so much as a passing word. I will never refer to it again. If I were dead, that could not be surer than it is henceforth. In the hour of my death, I shall hold sacred the one good remembrance – and shall thank and bless you for it – that

Sydney Carton Tells Lucie He Loves Her (continued)

my last avowal of myself was made to you, and that my name, and faults, and miseries were gently carried in your heart. May it otherwise be light and happy!'

He was so unlike what he had ever shown himself to be, and it was so sad to think how much he had thrown away, and how much he every day kept down and perverted, that Lucie Manette wept mournfully for him as he stood looking back at her.

'Be comforted!' he said, 'I am not worth such feeling, Miss Manette. An hour or two hence, and the low companions and low habits that I scorn but yield to, will render me less worth such tears as those, than any wretch who creeps along the streets. Be comforted! But, within myself, I shall always be, towards you, what I am now, though outwardly I shall be what you have heretofore seen me. The last supplication but one I make to you, is, that you will believe this of me.'

'I will, Mr Carton.' She was pale and trembling.

'My last supplication of all, is this; and with it, I will relieve you of a visitor with whom I well know you have nothing in unison, and between whom and you there is an impassable space. It is useless to say it, I know, but it rises out of my soul. For you, and for any dear to you, I would do anything. If my career were of that better kind that there was any opportunity or capacity of sacrifice in it, I would embrace any sacrifice for you and for those dear to you. Try to hold me in your mind, at some quiet times, as ardent and sincere in this one thing. The time will come, the time will not be long in coming, when new ties will be formed about you – ties that will bind you yet more tenderly and strongly to the home you so adorn – the dearest ties that will ever grace and gladden you. O Miss Manette, when the little picture of a happy father's face looks up in yours, when you see your own bright beauty springing up anew at your feet, think now and then that there is a man who would give his life, to keep a life you love beside you!'

He said, 'Farewell!' Said a last, 'God bless you!' and left her.

19 Codes (large group)

When sides are at war they need secret signals or codes to send messages to friends and protect against enemies. This spy, Madame Defarge, uses the secret signal of a rose to warn of danger. Choose a volunteer to go out of the room. Then agree on a code: for example, all people with long hair stand on one side of the room, or everyone has to cross their legs. When the volunteer returns he or she has to guess the code.

20 The revelation (pairs)

The Defarges who sheltered Dr Manette after he came out of prison, are spies for the Revolution, working with other citizens to overthrow the aristocracy. In her incessant knitting, Madame Defarge lists the names of people who will die on the guillotine. She wears a rose when a stranger is present in the wineshop to warn her comrades not to speak freely.

- Make notes on the news she hears about Dr Manette and his daughter.
- Why is this news so terrible?
- What do you think could happen next?

The Wine Shop

The story returns to Paris. The Defarges run a wine shop which is a spy centre for the French Revolutionaries. They are dismayed to hear that Lucie has married Charles Darnay who we now find out is the nephew of the Marquis described on page 109. He is therefore an aristocrat and their enemy They hope that neither Lucie nor her new husband will return to France.

A figure entering at the door threw a shadow on Madame Defarge which she felt to be a new one. She laid down her knitting, and began to pin her rose in her head-dress, before she looked at the figure.

It was curious. The moment Madame Defarge took up the rose, the customers ceased talking, and began gradually to drop out of the wine-shop.

'Good day, madame,' said the newcomer.

'Good day, monsieur.'

She said it aloud, but added to herself, as she resumed her knitting: 'Hah! Good day, age about forty, height about five feet nine, black hair, generally rather handsome visage, complexion dark, eyes dark, thin long and sallow face, aquiline nose but not straight, having a peculiar inclination towards the left cheek which imparts a sinister expression! Good day, one and all!'

'Have the goodness to give me a little glass of old cognac, and a mouthful of cool fresh water, madame.'

Madame complied with a polite air and took up her knitting.

The visitor watched her fingers for a few moments, and took the opportunity of observing the place in general.

'You knit with great skill, madame.'

'I am accustomed to it.'

'A pretty pattern too!'

'*You* think so?' said madame, looking at him with a smile.

'Decidedly. May one ask what it is for?'

'Pastime,' said madame, still looking at him with a smile, while her fingers moved nimbly.

'Not for use?'

'That depends. I may find a use for it one day. If I do – well,' said madame, drawing a breath and nodding her head with a stern kind of coquetry, 'I'll use it!'

It was remarkable; but the taste of Saint Antoine seemed to be decidedly opposed to a rose on the head-dress of Madame Defarge. Two men had entered separately, and had been about to order drink, when, catching sight of that novelty, they faltered, made a pretence of looking about as if for some friend who was not there, and went away. Nor, of those who had been there when this visitor entered, was there one left. They had all dropped off. The spy had kept his eyes open, but had been able to detect no sign. They had lounged away in a poverty-stricken, purposeless, accidental manner, quite natural and unimpeachable.

CONTINUED ☞

The Wine Shop (continued)

'John,' thought madame, checking off her work as her fingers knitted, and her eyes looked at the stranger. 'Stay long enough, and I shall knit "*Barsad*" before you go.'

'Business seems bad?'

'Business is very bad; the people are so poor.'

'Ah, the unfortunate, miserable people! So oppressed, too – as you say.'

'As *you* say,' madame retorted, correcting him, and deftly knitting an extra something into his name that boded him no good.

'Pardon me; certainly it was I who said so, but you naturally think so. Of course.'

'*I* think?' returned madame, in a high voice. 'I and my husband have enough to do to keep this wine-shop open, without thinking. All we think, here, is how to live. That is the subject *we* think of, and it gives us, from morning to night, enough to think about, without embarrassing our heads concerning others. *I* think for others? No, no.'

'You seem to know this quarter well; that is to say, better than I do?' observed Monsieur Defarge.

'Not at all, but I hope to know it better. I am so profoundly interested in its miserable inhabitants.'

'Hah!' muttered Defarge.

'The pleasure of conversing with you, Monsieur Defarge, recalls to me,' pursued the spy, 'that I have the honour of cherishing some interesting associations with your name.'

'Indeed!' said Defarge, with much indifference.

'Yes, indeed. When Dr Manette was released, you, his old domestic, had the charge of him, I know. He was delivered to you. You see I am informed of the circumstances?'

'Such is the fact, certainly,' said Defarge.

'It was to you,' said the spy, 'that his daughter came; and it was from your care that his daughter took him, accompanied by a neat brown monsieur; how is he called? – in a little wig – Lorry – of the bank of Tellson and Company – over to England.'

'Such is the fact,' repeated Defarge.

'Very interesting remembrances!' said the spy. 'I have known Dr Manette and his daughter, in England.'

'Yes?' said Defarge.

After sipping his cognac to the end, the spy added:

'Yes, Miss Manette is going to be married. But not to an Englishman; to one who, like herself, is French by birth. It is a curious thing that she is going to marry the nephew of Monsieur the Marquis. But he lives unknown in England, he is no Marquis there; he is Mr Charles Darnay. D'Aulnais is the name of his mother's family.'

Madame Defarge knitted steadily, but the intelligence had a palpable effect upon

The Wine Shop (continued)

her husband. Do what he would, behind the little counter, as to the striking of a light and the lighting of his pipe, he was troubled, and his hand was not trustworthy. The spy would have been no spy if he had failed to see it, or to record it in his mind.

Having made, at least, this one hit, Mr Barsad paid for what he had drunk, and took his leave.

For some minutes after he had emerged into the outer presence of Saint Antoine, the husband and wife remained exactly as he had left them, lest he should come back.

'Can it be true,' said Defarge, in a low voice, looking down at his wife as he stood smoking with his hand on the back of her chair: 'what he has said of Ma'amselle Manette?'

'As he has said it,' returned madame, lifting her eyebrows a little, 'it is probably false. But it may be true.'

'If it is –' Defarge began, and stopped.

'If it is?' repeated his wife.

'– And if it does come, while we live to see it triumph – I hope, for her sake, Destiny will keep her husband out of France.'

'Her husband's destiny,' said Madame Defarge, with her usual composure, 'will take him where he is to go, and will lead him to the end that is to end him. That is all I know.'

'But it is very strange – now, at least, is it not very strange' – said Defarge, rather pleading with his wife to induce her to admit it, 'that, after all our sympathy for Monsieur her father, and herself, her husband's name should be proscribed under your hand at this moment, by the side of that infernal dog's who has just left us?'

'Stranger things than that will happen when it does come,' answered madame. 'I have them both here, of a certainty; and they are both here for their merits; that is enough.'

She rolled up her knitting when she had said those words, and presently took the rose out of the handkerchief that was wound about her head.

In the evening, Madame Defarge with her work in her hand was accustomed to pass from place to place and from group to group. All the women knitted. They knitted worthless things; but the mechanical work was a mechanical substitute for eating and drinking; the hands moved for the jaws and the digestive apparatus: if the bony fingers had been still, the stomachs would have been more famine-pinched.

But, as the fingers went, the eyes went, and the thoughts. And as Madame Defarge moved on from group to group, all three went quicker and fiercer among every little knot of women that she had spoken with, and left behind.

Her husband smoked at his door, looking after her with admiration. 'A great woman,' said he, 'a strong woman, a grand woman, a frightfully grand woman!'

21 A loss of perspective (individual)

The passage opposite describes the frenzy of the common people in Paris.
They are sharpening their knives in a central courtyard, and killing
aristocrats in the city. Activity 2 on page 98 explored how Dickens uses
antithesis (opposites) to show the reader the difficulty of making clear
judgements. This passage encourages the reader to form a judgement by
using different techniques. Draw a column plan similar to the one below.
Then go on to fill in the methods Dickens uses.

Technique Dickens uses	Evidence of this technique	Effect
Repeated references to blood		
Appeal to the senses	'the whirling of the grindstone' (hearing)	The reader hears the sound. It seems chaotic and overwhelming.
Multiple sentences made up of phrases joined together with constant repetition		
Exclamatory sentences		

22 Justified violence? (pairs)

Why did the people behave so aggressively?

Look back at page 109 which tells you about the attitude of the Marquis, and
then write a paragraph from the viewpoint of the characters pictured here.
In your account, explain why you are so angry and out for aristocratic blood.

The Grindstone

The atmosphere in Paris is becoming even more brutal. The citizens are in a courtyard, sharpening their knives ready to kill the aristocrats. Murder has stirred the crowd to a frenzy.

The window looked out upon a throng of men and women: not enough in number, or near enough, to fill the courtyard: not more than forty or fifty in all. The people in possession of the house had let them in at the gate, and they had rushed in to work at the grindstone; it had evidently been set up there for their purpose, as in a convenient and retired spot.

But, such awful workers, and such awful work!

The grindstone had a double handle, and turning at it madly were two men, whose faces, as their long hair flapped back when the whirlings of the grindstone brought their faces up, were more horrible and cruel than the visages of the wildest savages in their most barbarous disguise. False eyebrows and false moustaches were stuck upon them, and their hideous countenances were all bloody and sweaty, and all awry with howling, and all staring and glaring with beastly excitement and want of sleep. As these ruffians turned and turned, their matted locks now flung forward over their eyes, now flung backward over their necks, some women held wine to their mouths that they might drink; and what with dropping blood, and what with dropping wine, and what with the stream of sparks struck out of the stone, all their wicked atmosphere seemed gore and fire. The eye could not detect one creature in the group free from the smear of blood. Shouldering one another to get next at the sharpening-stone, were men stripped to the waist, with the stain all over their limbs and bodies; men in all sorts of rags, with the stain upon those rags; men devilishly set off with spoils of women's lace and silk and ribbon, with the stain dyeing those trifles through and through. Hatchets, knives, bayonets, swords, all brought to be sharpened, were all red with it. Some of the hacked swords were tied to the wrists of those who carried them, with strips of linen and fragments of dress: ligatures various in kind, but all deep of the one colour.

The Switch

Charles Darnay returns to Paris and is arrested and imprisoned by the Revolutionaries. Lucie follows him with her father and Sydney Carton. They try to rescue him by legal means but he is sentenced to the guillotine. Sydney Carton knows it will destroy Lucie's happiness if Charles Darnay dies, and decides that since his own life is worthless to him, he will take Darnay's place. He bribes the Spy to take him to the cell where Charles Darnay is awaiting execution.

Footsteps in the stone passage outside the door. He stopped.

The key was put in the lock, and turned. Before the door was opened, or as it opened, a man said in a low voice, in English: 'He has never seen me here; I have kept out of his way. Go you in alone; I wait near. Lose no time!'

The door was quickly opened and closed, and there stood before him face to face, quiet, intent upon him, with the light of a smile on his features, and a cautionary finger on his lip, Sydney Carton.

There was something so bright and remarkable in his look, that, for the first moment, the prisoner misdoubted him to be an apparition of his own imagining. But, he spoke, and it was his voice; he took the prisoner's hand, and it was his real grasp.

'Of all the people upon earth, you least expected to see me?' he said.

'I could not believe it to be you. I can scarcely believe it now. You are not' – the apprehension came suddenly into his mind – 'a prisoner?'

'No. I am accidentally possessed of a power over one of the keepers here, and in virtue of it I stand before you. I come from her – your wife, dear Darnay.'

The prisoner wrung his hand.

'I bring you a request from her.'

'What is it?'

'A most earnest, pressing, and emphatic entreaty, addressed to you in the most pathetic tones of the voice so dear to you, that you well remember.'
The prisoner turned his face partly aside.

'You have no time to ask me why I bring it, or what it means; I have no time to tell you. You must comply with it – take off those boots you wear, and draw on these of mine.'

There was a chair against the wall of the cell, behind the prisoner. Carton, pressing forward, had already, with the speed of lightning, got him down into it, and stood over him, barefoot.

'Draw on these boots of mine. Put your hands to them; put your will to them. Quick!'

'Carton, there is no escaping from this place; it never can be done. You will only die with me. It is madness.'

'It would be madness if I asked you to escape; but do I? When I ask you to pass out at that door, tell me it is madness and remain here. Change that cravat for this of

CONTINUED ☞

The Switch (continued)

mine, that coat for this of mine. While you do it, let me take this ribbon from your hair, and shake out your hair like this of mine!'

With wonderful quickness, and with a strength both of will and action, that appeared quite supernatural, he forced all these changes upon him. The prisoner was like a young child in his hands.

'Carton! Dear Carton! It is madness. It cannot be accomplished, it never can be done, it has been attempted, and has always failed. I implore you not to add your death to the bitterness of mine.'

'Do I ask you, my dear Darnay, to pass the door? When I ask that, refuse. There are pen and ink and paper on this table. Is your hand steady enough to write?'

'It was when you came in.'

'Steady it again, and write what I shall dictate. Quick, friend, quick!'

Pressing his hand to his bewildered head, Darnay sat down at the table, Carton, with his right hand in his pocket, stood close beside him.

'Write exactly as I speak.'

'To whom do I address it?'

'To no one.' Carton still had his hand in his pocket.

'Do I date it?'

'No.'

The prisoner looked up, at each question. Carton, standing over him with his hand in his pocket, looked down.

'"If you remember,"' said Carton, dictating, '"the words that passed between us, long ago, you will readily comprehend this when you see it. You do remember them, I know. It is not in your nature to forget them."'

He was drawing his hand from his pocket, the prisoner chancing to look up in his hurried wonder as he wrote, the hand stopped, closing upon something.

'Have you written "forget them"?' Carton asked.

'I have. Is that a weapon in your hand?'

'No; I am not armed.'

'What is it in your hand?'

'You shall know directly. Write on; there are but a few words more.' He dictated again. '"I am thankful that the time has come, when I can prove them. That I do so is no subject for regret or grief."' As he said these words with his eyes fixed on the writer, his hand slowly and softly moved down close to the writer's face.

The pen dropped from Darnay's fingers on the table, and he looked about him vacantly.

'What vapour is that?' he asked

'Vapour?'

'Something that crossed me?'

'I am conscious of nothing; there can be nothing here. Take up the pen and finish. Hurry, hurry!'

The Switch (continued)

The prisoner bent over the paper, once more.

'"If it had been otherwise;"' Carton's hand was again watchfully and softly stealing down; '"I never should have used the longer opportunity. If it had been otherwise;"' the hand was at the prisoner's face; '"I should but have had so much the more to answer for. If it had been otherwise —"' Carton looked at the pen and saw it was trailing off into unintelligible signs.

Carton's hand moved back no more. The prisoner sprang up with a reproachful look, but Carton's hand was close and firm at his nostrils, and Carton's left arm caught him round the waist. For a few seconds he faintly struggled with the man who had come to lay down his life for him; but, within a minute or so, he was stretched insensible on the ground.

Quickly, but with hands as true to the purpose as his heart was, Carton dressed himself in the clothes the prisoner had laid aside, combed back his hair, and tied it with the ribbon the prisoner had worn. Then, he softly called, 'Enter there! Come in!' and the spy presented himself.

'You see?' said Carton, looking up, as he kneeled on one knee beside the insensible figure, putting the paper in a pocket: 'Is your hazard very great?'

'Mr Carton,' the spy answered, with a timid snap of his fingers, 'my hazard is not *that*, in the thick of business here, if you are true to the whole of your bargain.'

'Don't fear me. I will be true to the death.'

'You must be, Mr Carton.'

'Have no fear! I shall soon be out of the way of harming you, and the rest will soon be far from here, please God! Now, get assistance and take me to the coach.'

'You?' said the spy nervously.

'Him, man, with whom I have exchanged. You go out at the gate by which you brought me in?'

'Of course.'

'I was weak and faint when you brought me in, and I am fainter now you take me out. The parting interview has overpowered me. Such a thing has happened here, often, and too often. Your life is in your own hands. Quick! Call assistance!'

'You swear not to betray me?' said the trembling spy, as he paused for a last moment.

'Man, man!' returned Carton, stamping his foot; 'have I sworn by no solemn vow already, to go through with this, that you waste the precious moments now? Take him yourself to the courtyard you know of, place him yourself in the carriage, show him yourself to Mr Lorry, tell him yourself to give him no restorative but air, and to remember my words of last night, and his promise of last night, and drive away!'

The spy withdrew, and Carton seated himself at the table, resting his forehead on his hands. The spy returned immediately, with two men.

They raised the unconscious figure, placed it on a litter they had brought to the door, and bent to carry it away.

CONTINUED ☞

23 Sacrifice (small groups)

Darnay returns to Paris and is imprisoned by the Revolutionaries because he is the Marquis' nephew. Carton decides to switch places with him because his own life seems worthless to him, since Lucie does not love him. This is Carton's opportunity to help Lucie by saving her husband Darnay. Carton knows Darnay will not agree to his sacrificing his life. Make notes on how Carton achieves his aims.

24 Interviewing Darnay and Carton (groups of three)

Imagine that Darnay and Carton are caught by the prison authorities before the switch. The prison governor interviews them separately. Before your interview prepare to answer on the following topics:

- what I did with my life
- mistakes I made
- how I feel
- last wishes.

25 What makes *A Tale of Two Cities* a heroic tragedy? (pairs)

Identify *heroism* (behaving in a courageous way to help another) and *tragedy* (death or disaster which happens to a character or characters) in the following aspects of the novel:

- character
- plot
- setting.

For example:
Carton's action in choosing to go to his death for another could be called heroic because …

The Switch (continued)

'The time is short, Evrémonde,' said the spy, in a warning voice.

The door closed, and Carton was left alone. Straining his powers of listening to the utmost, he listened for any sound that might denote suspicion or alarm. There was none. Keys turned, doors clashed, footsteps passed along distant passages: no cry was raised, or hurry made, that seemed unusual. Breathing more freely in a little while, he sat down at the table, and listened again until the clock struck two.

Sounds that he was not afraid of, for he divined their meaning, then began to be audible. Several doors opened in succession and finally his own. A gaoler, with a list in his hand, looked in, merely saying, 'Follow me, Evrémonde!' and he followed into a large dark room, at a distance. It was a dark winter day, and what with the shadows within, and what with the shadows without, he could but dimly discern the others who were brought there to have their arms bound. Some were standing; some seated. Some were lamenting, and in restless motion; but these were few. The great majority were silent and still, looking fixedly at the ground. As he stood by the wall in a dim corner, while some of the fifty-two were brought in after him, a young woman, with a slight girlish form, a sweet spare face in which there was no vestige of colour, and large widely opened patient eyes, rose from the seat where he had observed her sitting, and came to speak to him.

'Citizen Evrémonde,' she said, touching him with her cold hand, 'I am a poor little seamstress, who was with you in La Force.'

As the last thing on earth that his heart was to warm and soften to, it warmed and softened to this pitiable girl.

'I heard you were released, Citizen Evrémonde. I hoped it was true?'

'It was. But, I was again taken and condemned.'

'If I may ride with you, Citizen Evrémonde, will you let me hold your hand? I am not afraid, but I am little and weak, and it will give me more courage.'

As the patient eyes were lifted to his face, he saw a sudden doubt in them, and then astonishment. He pressed the work-worn, hunger-worn young fingers, and touched his lips.

'Are you dying for him?' she whispered.

'And his wife and child. Hush! Yes.'

'O you will let me hold your brave hand, stranger?'

'Hush! Yes, my poor sister; to the last.'

And Finally ...

To discuss (groups of six)

- Which novel did you like best, and why?
- Which characters did you like best and least? Give your reasons.
- Choose your favourite episode.

Creative response (pairs)

Aspects of Dickens' writing will have become clearer to you as you read the extracts from some of his books. Draw a column plan similar to this one, on which you collect information about Dickens' style.

Technique Dickens uses and its effect	Example from story
Repetition of phrases for emphasis	Page 77 in *Great Expectations* shows ... Page 99 in *A Tale of Two Cities* shows ...
Pathetic fallacy (scenes reflecting a character's feelings)	
Antithesis (opposites)	

Using some of Dickens' techniques, write your own story about

- a character
- a place
- an adventure.

Literary response (pairs)

- How do *Great Expectations* and *A Tale of Two Cities* demonstrate the characteristics of an adventure story?
- How do *A Christmas Carol* and *Oliver Twist* give the reader a chance to reflect on past actions?